Adventures of a Yiddish Lecturer

Adventures of a Yiddish Lecturer

Abraham Shulman

The Pilgrim Press

New York

Library of Congress Cataloging in Publication Data
Shulman, Abraham.
    Adventures of a Yiddish lecturer.

    1. Jews in the United States—Anecdotes, facetiae, satire, etc.
2. Shulman, Abraham—Anecdotes. 3. Lecturers—United States—Anecdotes, facetiae, satire, etc. 4. United States—Anecdotes, facetiae,
satire, etc. I. Title.
E184.J5S49   973'.04924   79-28734
ISBN 0-8298-0391-2

The Pilgrim Press, 132 W. 31 Street, New York, New York 10001

CONTENTS

INTRODUCTION

Abraham Shulman is the author of several books of satirical essays; he also writes literary criticism. He was previously the editor of a Jewish daily in Paris, and now writes for the "Jewish Daily Forward." I always read his column with great pleasure. He is blessed with a rare humor.

As a Yiddish lecturer in this country, Abraham Shulman has had the opportunity to come in direct contact with the first generation of Jewish immigrants, and to observe all the traits and idiosyncrasies that mark their characters.

The Yiddish immigrant was often uneducated, but was almost always complex and full of inconsistencies. He came to this "golden land" with the conviction that the United States was a melting pot in which ethnic groups must give up their individualities and become 100% Americans—and at the same time believed in an International which would transcend all national and political boundaries and unite all mankind with a single bond. Various leftist theoreticians and utopians of all sorts fed the immigrant their false systems and convictions, but the life he encountered hit him with merciless reality. Whatever the immigrant had imagined, whatever he had hoped for, was rebutted with its opposite.

It isn't easy to lecture to such people. They ask countless questions; they're full of just and imagined claims and grudges. They're disappointed by a world which didn't follow the plans which their leaders had mapped out. They are always pathetic, often tragic, and frequently comical.

"The Adventures of a Yiddish Lecturer" gives the reader a perception of the lives of these last holdovers of a vanishing life and culture. Many are bundles of contradictions: they are internationalistic and Zionistic, religious and atheistic, pacifist and militant fighters (at least in their hearts) for the Jewish homeland. Despite the fact that they continuously talk about progress, they all live in the past. Their lives have been such that they feel the pains of the human race more sharply than any other group.

Abraham Shulman's book is more than a collection of episodes; it's an insight into the lives and thoughts of these people. There are few Yiddish satirists like Abraham Shulman, with such a sense of sharpness, and also human warmth. I recommend this book to all who are interested in the greatest adventure of adventures: of the human and Jewish individuality.

Isaac Bashevis Singer

Author's Foreword

I came to the United States from the French port of Le Havre on a Friday afternoon. I arrived on a boat as a regular immigrant with my family—wife and two children who, several days later, I started to call "kids." The year was 1960 and this arrival to the port of New York had nothing of the color, the poetry, or the misery of the Ellis Island arrivals two generations earlier. I had come on the invitation of the Yiddish newspaper "The Jewish Daily Forward," which at that time still had 80,000 readers and over 60 writers, to join the staff.

My first disappointment was of a financial nature: the salary of a Forward writer was hardly sufficient to sustain a family of four. Fortunately, during a welcome party organized by a group of colleagues, during which I gave a short speech on Jewish life in Europe, a man said to me: "You have the tongue of a speaker. It's a gold mine." He was the head of a Jewish organization which had branches all over the country. He addressed me as "Genosse," the German word for "comrade" retained by the socialist old-timers in this country. "I liked your talk," he said, "I'm going to put your name on our list of speakers who give lectures to Yiddish speaking audiences."

We met the next day in the cafeteria next to the old Forward building in the Lower East Side, over two huge cups of coffee and equally large cheesecake slices. The saltshakers were so large that I thought them to contain sugar and mixed two spoonfuls into my coffee. My companion watched me bewildered. Did he think that this was the way people drink coffee in the capital of cultural France? I took a bite of the cake and followed it with a gulp from the cup. I began to cough. I had another swift gulp of coffee to suppress the taste of the cake. I felt horrible. I pushed away the cake saying: "What a strange pastry." "It isn't the pastry," the man said gently. "You've put salt into your coffee." At the sound of the word "salt" I jumped up from the chair and ran into the men's room. When I came back there was a cup of fresh coffee and a slice of strudel. For some reason this episode changed our acquaintance into a years-long friendship.

The man—his name was Nochum Chanin—informed me that his organization had a number of lecturers, all of them prominent writers and scholars. He gave me a small, green booklet containing the names of the speakers in alphabetical order together with the subjects of their talks.

Mr. Chanin was a remarkable man—warm, wise, simple—a "folksmentch." I still remember his instructions: "Don't ever talk down to the audience—they may know less than you do, but most of them are smarter than you are and, very often unpredictable. You may be a college professor with a dozen diplomas; to them you are a greenhorn, an inferior species. Start your lecture with a joke, even when it is about a national catastrophe. Be personal, tell them where you come from—you cannot compete with their status as 'Amerikaner', but you can ingratiate yourself as a descendant from a shtetl. Use a simple language, avoid words of three or more syllables, but don't be too simple either. If the lecture is too easy, they will afterwards say: "It wasn't worth a penny, I understood every word." It's better to hear them say: "The lecture was profound, I didn't understand half of it." Don't be too controversial, most of them prefer a speaker who agrees with their convictions; don't be too opportunistic either—they'll treat you with chutzpah. The man to reckon with most is the chairman; he was put there not for your glory but for his own. Don't object when he compares you to Albert Einstein or Bertrand Russell, he doesn't mean that you are a mathematician or a philosopher, he is just announcing that he is aware of such names. Some of the chairmen may use the introduction as a vehicle for their own lecture. Don't show impatience. You are only a passing visitor—he is there to stay and he must show a reason why the members should elect him for another term."

I said to him: "Thank you for the advice. I will certainly remember it." "I haven't finished," Mr. Chanin said. "You must keep in mind that a lecture will very seldom be the only attraction; more often it will be a supplement to a membership meeting or to a family celebration. Also, each of the lectures will have an artistic supplement—a performance of a singer, fiddle-player or even a magician. You'll be sitting at the praesidium table, so clap in such a way that everyone can see it; you'll be watched by the performer's family. After each lecture there is a question period. Let no question astonish you—it's quite possible that after a talk on literature you will get a question about the life span of an elephant. Don't show surprise, answer it straight and loud."

"Thank you again, Mr. Chanin."

"Don't mention it. And now go home and write down the titles of your proposed lectures."

A few weeks later I joined the band of lecturers and began roaming the country, visiting the big cities, townships and small settlements. I spoke to gatherings of many hundreds, and to groups of no more than a dozen, on such subjects as Yiddish literature, folklore and Jewish humor. Anybody who has ever had anything to do with the profession of teaching knows the truth that the teacher often gets out of his audience more than the audience does from the teacher. My lecturing was a rewarding experience. I was given the chance to meet an exciting category of people, all of whom belonged to the first generation of immigrants who had come to this "golden land" hoping to become instant "Amerikaner" but trying at the same time with all their force not to relinquish the values imported from the shtetl.

From the very beginning I felt an urge to mark down my impressions; I soon realized how limited was my gift to bring across the richness and vitality of these experiences. I resigned myself to a smaller task—to deal with the less serious sides of the subject in the hope that others, more equipped, will use this material as a stimulus to more ambitious attempts.

The stories in this book—sometimes no more than brief episodes—are fragments of an entity with a common plot and with a common cast: the chairman, a man with almost dictatorial powers; his entourage of executive members, who have the dignity of cabinet ministers; the colorful, live, alert and always exciting audience. The speaker himself, who should be the protagonist of the show, very often was no more than a marginal extra.

I still have the small green booklet which Mr. Chanin gave me at our first encounter. Now, fifteen years later, most of the speakers have "gathered unto their ancestors," and so has the great majority of the audiences. Soon—the remainder will inevitably follow their footsteps. May this book succeed in retaining at least a momentary glimpse into the lives of these remarkable people.

A.S.

THE MISSION OF JEWISH HUMOR

A small Jewish community in New York invited me to lecture on Jewish humor. I boarded a bus in the Port Authority building carrying a small briefcase—an old European habit. I kept my lecture notes inside as well as several books which I used during the talk to illustrate some points.

The theory I was planning to expound was quite flattering to my audience. I maintained that not only were the Jewish people possessed of the sharpest and most refined sense of humor, but that Jewish wit was at the root of the geneological tree of the universe. As opposed to the theory that Jewish laughter is tearful, I collected enough material to prove that its nucleus is one of optimism and hilarity. This lecture was usually a success since my audiences liked the idea of being the progenitors of cosmopolitan wit. Besides offering this satisfaction, the lecture contained many Jewish sayings, chochmes, and jokes which usually evoked cascades of laughter from the listeners.

The bus arrived on time and after receiving instructions from several passers-by, I found the building with a Yiddish sign bearing the name of the organization. The

1

door was open and I crossed a long, narrow passage to find myself in a large meeting hall.

There were about a hundred chairs arranged more or less in rows. All the chairs were empty except for one in the center which was occupied by an elderly man in a gray winter coat and a heavy cap. He sat motionless and listened attentively to what was being said at the rostrum. Facing the door stood a long table covered with a green cloth and sitting around it were seven elderly gentlemen, apparently the society's executive board.

As I opened the door, all of the gentlemen raised their heads and gave me a curious look. One of them, who sat at the corner of the table over a big ledger, shouted at me:

"What do you want?"

The only way to answer was either to walk over to the table or to shout from where I stood at the door. I decided to shout: "I'm the lecturer from New York." The man with the ledger, no doubt the secretary, turned to the redheaded chairman: "Shall we let him in?"

The chairman looked at me with cold indifference and said to his fellow officers: "He can, if he wants to, sit down and wait until we finish the general meeting."

I sat down on the nearest chair. After a little while, I realized that I had arrived in the middle of a heated debate. The subject was the problem of the cemetery lots which belonged to the organization. The question was a crucial one. Several members of the community, who were not members of the organization, had applied for the privilege of being buried, after their 120 years, in the society's plots. The officers however, were sharply divided among themselves, and the president was absolutely against it.

"Never!" he said. "We shall never allow people who did not belong to us while they were alive to come to us after they die and lie in our graves. They who have not planted shall not reap."

Then the vice-president, who sat at his right asked for the floor. He sprang to his feet, a round faced man with gray hair, and spoke in a mild but firm voice.

"Gentlemen," he said, "I can't see why we should be so harsh and uncompromising toward our brethren. All they want is one little thing, that we bury them in our midst. I don't see why we should refuse it. They want to rest in our plots? Fine. Let them. They are not going to bite us."

The word "bite" was the cue for a new eruption from the chairman. His face became almost green with scorn.

"It's not," he said, "a question of biting. Nobody is afraid of their bites. If they bite, we can bite back."

The secretary shared the president's point of view completely.

"I am of the same opinion as the chairman. People who did not think it fit to share our duties during their lives, are not going to enjoy privileges of membership at their death." He finished his verdict with a Yiddish idiom: "Let them take their feet over their shoulders and scram."

The scales were again weighted against the president. The treasurer now rose to face the audience: "I am of the opinion that we should treat the applicants with more understanding and friendliness. What is it they want? To be buried with us? By all means. With the greatest of pleasure!"

The president's face turned livid. The split was now too sharp to be resolved by the usual arguments. What was necessary at this point was decisiveness, and this was supplied by the secretary. He pulled out a sheet of paper from a drawer and held it over the heads of his colleagues.

"The question," he said, "is not whether we should or should not. The question is altogether different. Can we afford it? Can we be so generous and give away graves to others? Have we got enough for ourselves? And the answer," here he pointed his finger to the paper, "is no.

3

And why no? Because we have hardly enough for ourselves. It would be a grave injustice if we had to squeeze ourselves in order to let in outsiders."

The secretary's last words seemed to be final. Surely if the number of graves was hardly sufficient for the long-standing members, what chance could there be for those who did not even carry a membership card? But the debate was far from being concluded. The vice-president rose slowly from his chair.

"Gentlemen," he said mildly, "I am not going to claim that we have an overabundance of graves. I agree that we have enough of our members to fill every grave. But under what condition? Under the condition that all those who belong to our organization will actually be brought to our plots. But this is hardly the case. There are many among us who belong to several other societies at the same time and it is not at all certain that they will be buried in our section. I therefore suggest that a special subcommittee be appointed to conduct an investigation among the members to demand a clear answer to the question: Do you or don't you want to be buried with us?"

The president decided to demand a vote. "Those who are in favor of burying strangers in our midst, let them raise their hands."

The elderly man in the overcoat and fluffy cap didn't move.

"Who is against it?"

Again the gentleman remained still. The secretary then announced that since the general meeting had not decided one way or the other, the matter would be submitted to the special cemetery subcommittee. With this problem at least temporarily solved, the president banged the gavel on the table.

"We have many more items to cover concerning the cemetery department, but I move to postpone them till the end of the meeting. In the meantime, our distinguished lecturer from New York will give us a talk on Jewish humor. Let's hear him out and we shall then return to the remaining items on the agenda."

I stood up and started walking across the room clutching my briefcase under one arm. The floor squeaked and I tried to walk on my toes. When I finally reached the table, the seven officers crowded together and made room for me in the center, next to the chairman. I shook hands with everybody around the table, starting with the chairman, and then with all the rest.

The chairman got up. "Friends," he said, "we have now come to our next item, the lecture. I hope that our friend from New York who has been sitting for the last half hour in the audience, is acquainted with the fact that we still have some other points on the agenda and he will be as brief as is humanly possible."

Only the vice-president clapped when I rose to speak, but even before I said, "Thank you, Mr. Chairman," the elderly man in the audience also stood up and began to leave. The president looked at him scornfully:

"Mr. Blaustein, where do you think you are going?"

"I'm going home," said Mr. Blaustein, and he pulled down the flaps of his cap over his ears.

"But the meeting isn't over," said the chairman, "we are going to hear a lecture."

"I didn't come for no lectures," said Mr. Blaustein. "I came to hear about the cemetery."

"We all came to hear about the cemetery," said the chairman, "but we also have obligations toward our Jewish culture. The debate on the cemetery isn't finished, and as soon as this man briefly says what he has to say, he will catch his bus back to New York and we shall have all the time necessary to return to our subject."

Mr. Blaustein didn't seem convinced, but he submitted

to the discipline of the organization. He sat back in his chair, but he left the flaps of his cap where they were, over his ears.

That was the first time in my career as a lecturer that I abandoned the premise of the superiority of Jewish humor. Under pressure from the chairman, I also abandoned my customary practice of illustrating the lecture with Jewish jokes. The chairman held his hand over my books, and whenever I attempted to open one of them and read a joke aloud, he tightened his hold and said, "Let's stick to brass tacks."

After I finished, the chairman helped me put my notes and books back into the briefcase, and we again shook hands. On my way out, I saw Mr. Blaustein lift the hat flaps from his ears and settle down with renewed attention.

THE MAKING OF A LECTURE

The occasion was the Fiftieth Anniversary of the death of the Father of Modern Jewish Literature, Itzchok Leybush Peretz, or as he was affectionately called, "Yalperetz." The invitation to be a guest-speaker came from a town in Massachusetts. The train brought me there several hours early and one of the executive members who waited for me at the station brought me to the president's house. There I was to rest after the trip and at the same time get acquainted with the cultural leaders of the Jewish community.

The president was a small, plump man with a cloud of hair; he also had a heavy brown mustache and a pair of sad and penetrating eyes. In short, he looked like I. L. Peretz himself. The others in the room appeared less significant than their imposing chief executive, but only physically. They were all the intellectual cream of the community. One of them was a well-known literary critic. Another was a poet, not a Byron, but relatively popular in Yiddish-speaking circles. The third, the executive member who brought me from the station, was a less esteemed but prolific writer of Yiddish prose.

A few minutes after I shook hands with the four gentlemen, I was offered a cup of coffee with a plate of the most rotten cookies I ever tasted in a private home. The president settled himself in the center of the room and announced that they were going to work out the details of the evening. I didn't take down any notes of the debate but the following, to the best of my memory, is an honest reconstruction of the meeting.

"Gentlemen," said the president, "while our esteemed guest from New York relaxes after his trip and enjoys the homemade cookies of my missis, we'll work out the agenda of the evening. The plan is simplicity itself. The evening was announced for eight o'clock sharp and we shall not start later than 8:30. Considering the rules of the Community Center to evacuate the hall by 10:30, it follows that we agree on the round figure of two hours."

Everybody nodded.

"I suppose," here the president smiled most charmingly, "that nobody will have anything against my being chairman?"

The question was rhetorical; being the president of the organization he automatically was entitled to the chair. "As the head of the evening," he added, "I have prepared an introductory address of thirty-five minutes."

The others looked at each other with sullen faces. The literary critic, a rusty fellow with eyes protruding from behind horn-rimmed glasses, was more outspoken than the others. "Since when does the chairman's introduction take such a long time? Couldn't you shorten it?"

"Physically impossible," said the president, "my speech is divided into three parts: A general survey of the Jewish literature contemporary to Yalperetz; a brief evaluation of his importance; and a few words about our guest from New York. We mustn't forget that this is his first visit to our town and it will be more than proper to give him a hearty welcome."

"Alright," said the poet, who indeed looked like a poet:

he was tiny, fragile, with a thin platinum mustache, and delicate cheeks like butterfly wings. "After the president's introduction, I shall speak next and say what I have to say about the father of modern Jewish literature."

"How long?" asked the president.

"Thirty-five minutes."

The other two, the literary critic and the prose writer, an ascetic man with a bald head, gave him savage looks.

—How did you arrive at thirty-five minutes?—asked the critic.

—I checked it against a clock.

—You'll have to cut it—said the fiction writer in a whisper. But this was a whisper that could enter the marrow of the bones.

—Thirty-five minutes—said the poet—is after I have already cut it. Before cutting, it took over an hour.

The fiction writer narrowed his eyes to the size of two capsules of poison. "Considering that the chairman and the poet have appropriated for themselves an hour and ten minutes, how much time is left for reading my story?"

—How long is the story?—inquired the president.

—It should take an hour.

The critic chuckled. The poet turned his little head away in disgust. Only the chairman remained calm:

—You have to cut it.

—Mutilate a literary creation?

—Cut it—repeated the chairman.

—It will bleed.

—Cut it.

—The only thing I can do—said the fiction writer—is accelerate the tempo of reading. I'll have to read it with a galloping speed.

—Then go ahead and gallop—said the chairman and turned to the critic—How long are you willing to speak?

—Willing isn't the question. I could fill out the whole

evening and even then I wouldn't say one tenth of what I want to say about our great Peretz. But being faced with realities I shall speak no longer than all the rest: thirty-five minutes.

—Thirty-five minutes for what?—asked the fiction writer acidly.

—For saying a fraction of a fraction of what I, as a literary critic, have to say about our great Nobel Prize winner, I. L. Peretz.

—He never got the Nobel Prize—hissed the poet.

—Because of the anti-Semites in Stockholm.

The chairman intervened: "Gentlemen," he said, "our friend the critic is right. It's unthinkable to have an evening devoted to literature and not to listen to the one, who by the fact of his vocation is endowed with the gift of literary analysis."

The poet's butterfly cheeks became pink: "Where are we going to take an additional thirty-five minutes?"

—Where there's a will, there's a way—said the president (now, being a little excited, he looked more like Peretz than ever)—We'll have to squeeze and make room for the critic.

—I've shortened my speech by fifty percent—said the poet—I see no possible way of cutting it still further.

—As for me—said the fiction writer—I've already agreed to read my story with a double speed. If I accelerate it more, it will become completely incomprehensible.

—Gentlemen—said the president—we must girdle ourselves and try to be as realistic as is humanly possible. Let each of us cut seven minutes from his time; this will still leave everybody with an ample thirty minutes.

The poet looked away in gloom. The fiction writer's bald skull changed from a sickish grey to a moribund white. Only the president still retained his former spirit. He pulled at his voluminous mustache and said, marking it in a notebook: "There we are. It's all settled. I open the evening with an introduction of thirty minutes. Our friend the poet follows me with thirty. After him comes the fiction writer with thirty. And last but not least: the concise and Spartan analysis by our critic. We shall thus have a splendidly rich and diversified evening appropriate to the great and diverse figure of Yalperetz."

During all this time there was another person in the room who took no part in the debate, who moved discreetly around supplying everyone with her poisonous cookies. The president's wife, like her husband, had a solemn face with effulgent Semitic traits. In the interval, between one transport of cookies and another, she sat quietly on the edge of a chair listening reverently to the conversation. Now, after her husband had so adroitly summed up the plan for the evening, she opened her mouth for the first time.

"Gentlemen," she said, "haven't you forgotten something? What about the guest speaker from New York?"

A terrible silence followed her question. The four men looked in my direction. I was sitting in the corner of the room engulfed in a shroud of gloom. The president cried out: "My friends, we have all made a capital blunder. How do you like that?"

Nobody liked it. And nobody said a word. The president was suspended between the awareness of his duty and the horrible disposition of his colleagues. He tried a joke: "We could, of course, announce that the speaker hasn't arrived. That the train got stuck a hundred miles from here."

He giggled. Nobody joined him. He tried another joke: "We could also announce that our speaker arrived with a high fever. That he was taken for a checkup to Mount Sinai Hospital. We could suggest to the audience to send him the wish of a 'refuah shleyma'."

11

Again, nobody in the room gave as much as a snicker. The silence was dense and threatening. The literary critic broke it by saying obscurely: "This is hardly a time for jokes. If you remember, I was from the very start against inviting anybody from anywhere. We have enough talent of our own and there was no need to drag this gentleman all the way from New York. We needed it like a hole in the head. However, I was overvoted and loyally gave in. Now, since you have all cooked up the 'kashe', go ahead and eat it. I wash my hands."

He actually made a movement of washing his hands. The poet was of a different opinion: "We musn't wash our dirty linen in front of our esteemed guest. We have all agreed to invite him and we must bear the consequences."

—Right—said the president—Consequences is the right word. We must face the fact that the train hasn't broken down and that our guest has, thank God, not arrived with a high fever. The speaker is here and he has no less right to speak from the rostrum than anyone of us. Perhaps even more.

He scanned the other men's faces and they all turned away their heads. It was finally the critic, who until now had completely ignored my presence, who said to the president:

—Why don't you ask him how long he intends to speak?

—I was about to—said the president. He turned to me with hopeful anticipation—How long, considering everything you witnessed, do you plan to speak?

I said luridly: "One hour."

The poet, his cheeks now purple, snapped: "He's either a joker or else he enjoys drawing Jewish blood."

I opened my briefcase, took out a copy of the New York Yiddish newspaper and pointed to an advertisement: "This advertisement says clearly and with no ambiguities that the subject of the evening is: 'Fifty years after the death of I. L. Peretz' and that I, and here is my name printed with the same letters as those of Peretz, will be the speaker from New York. No other name is mentioned."

The president told me to hand him the paper and I complied with malice. He looked at it and his face flushed. He held out the newspaper before the faces of his colleagues: "What sort of an idiot gave this advertisement?"

The poet and the critic looked at the fiction writer who sat with a lowered head. The president sent him the gaze of a gangster: "You?"

—It was the decision of the committee. I was instructed to do it and I did it.

—You did it and you'll pay for it—said the president—You aren't going to open your mouth during the whole evening. Our esteemed guest from New York will speak on your time.

The fiction writer was as pale as a sheet. He took a knife from the plate of fruits and stretched out his neck: "Here," he said, "Go ahead and cut it."

This cooled the president's irritation. "Gentlemen," he said, "it's true that the fiction writer made a bloody mess in the way he formulated the advertisement. But he can't be made the scapegoat. Let's clarify the matter with our guest. He's had the opportunity of getting acquainted with all our perplexities and troubles. Let him therefore, after taking all this into consideration, say clearly how long he intends to speak."

"One hour," I said.

The president looked with despair at the others. The literary critic whispered: "He must be an Arab."

The poet got up from his chair and walked over to me. He put an arm around my shoulder: "My friend," he said, "we brought you all the way from New York. We covered the expenses. We booked you a room in one of the nicest hotels in town. After the evening you're invited to my house, to a very nice snack. Don't draw our blood; make it ten minutes and let it be settled."

"Let's give him fifteen," suggested the critic.

I looked at the four people in the room and their anguish began to break my heart. "Thirty minutes," I said and they could see that this was final.

"Gentlemen," said the president, "you can very well see with whom we have to deal. Let each of us give him seven minutes. Who is the first to go on Kidush Hashem?"

The poet stuck out his chest and said heroically: "I." The next on the sacrificial altar was the critic. Then followed the president. The only one to hesitate was the fiction writer but prompted by the looks of the others, he said with the voice of a suicide: "Take my seven minutes and—here he added a Yiddish curse—let it all go with the head to the ground."

The president gave a sigh of relief like a drowning man dragged from the bottom of a lake. "Gentlemen," he announced, "the operation was painful but the patient is alive. Everything as you can see is just dandy."

"Not everything," sounded the Cassandra voice of the president's wife. They all turned towards her. She was not only the provider of the pernicious cakes, she was also, for the second time, the bearer of bad tidings: "Have you forgotten about the folksinger Zenobius Katz?"

The president gasped: "It slipped my mind."

The fiction writer said sharply—his father must have been a ritual slaughterer: "I see no reason to worry. We'll simply cut him."

The poet giggled. Only a man who stands beneath his gallows could giggle like that: "Cut him? Zenobius Katz? The only male singer with a coloratura? Why do you think the people are coming? For our speeches. He's the hit of the evening."

14

—We can announce—suggested the critic—that the hit had a heart seizure.

—Impossible—said the poet—He's too much of an s.o.b. to cooperate. And secondly, how do you know that he isn't already there with his lame pianist? He always comes early to warm up his disgusting voice.

The atmosphere was macabre. The president's wife, who felt responsible for all the trouble, slipped out of the room. The president looked at the window. Was he contemplating suicide? From the ground floor? He said darkly: "There's no other way. We must squeeze again."

"Absolutely and categorically out of the question," said the critic and got up from his seat. "I have no intention of participating in any more discussions. I'll see you in the meeting hall."

The president grabbed him by a sleeve and pulled him back. "We shall resolve nothing by putting our heads in the sand. Zenobius Katz is in the program and no force on this earth can change this unpleasant fact. The only thing we can do is to appeal to him not to give any speeches before each song. If he does, we'll order the janitor to wheel out the piano in the middle of his singing. As for us, gentlemen, we must once more shorten our speeches."

"I've already arrived at the naked bones of my analysis," said the critic.

"One more cut," said the poet, "and my whole speech won't be worth a bent nickel."

The fiction writer again grabbed the knife from the table and stretched his neck: "Go ahead and cut it."

The president's eyes were fixed on me. His meaning was clear. Would I agree to get a 103 fever and let the audience send me wishes for a speedy recovery? I ignored his looks. The last and feeble suggestion came from the poet: "Granted that this Katz has to appear in the potpourri of his lousy songs, can't he be put in a corner of the room

15

where he can sing as much as he wants while we go on with our speeches?" No one took his suggestion seriously and the only remaining suggestion was to make further cuts.

Some fifteen minutes later we slipped into the president's black limousine and drove in silence to the Community Center.

Surprisingly, the evening was a success. The president started the business with his speech, which didn't exceed the allotted time by a single second. Then he began to interrupt the speeches of his colleagues with no trace of pity, in the middle of sentences. By coincidence they all had to stop after a question which they had no chance to answer. And so the poet was cut off after he asked poetically: "And what will the generations of the future learn from the teachings of our great I. L. Peretz?" The literary critic was stopped after he exclaimed: "And why do we call him the Father of Modern Jewish Literature?" The fiction writer read a symbolic story in which a young girl, representing the Jewish Nation, asks her lover, the symbol of Messiah: "Do you love me?" The public never found out whether he did or not, for the president pulled the writer away from the mike.

The male coloratura was warned before he went up on the rostrum that one minute too long and the piano together with the pianist would be wheeled out by the janitor. I was to conclude the evening. It wasn't necessary to give me any warnings; I was gently told that at exactly half past ten the administration of the building puts out the lights. Nevertheless, when I walked over to the lectern I found there a slip of paper with one word only: "Arab." But I spoke with more flair than ever before.

WHAT'S IN A NAME?

The subject this time was, "Social Elements in Jewish Humor." I had every reason to be satisfied. The audience was relatively large, and the chairman did everything he could to create an atmosphere of joviality. And yet, I returned home in a gloomy mood. I was upset because the chairman, in his few introductory words, had changed my name from Abraham to Boruch. "Ladies and Gentlemen," he said, "it is my great privilege to introduce the guest speaker of our program, Genosse Boruch Shulman." (Genosse means "Comrade").

For those who are acquainted with the history of the Jewish revolutionary movement in Eastern Europe, the name Boruch Shulman is no less familiar than that of Robespierre or Garibaldi. It was he who threw a bomb at one of the satraps during the bloody regime of the Russian Czars, and who was subsequently immortalized in song, folktale and legend for his heroism. Obviously the elderly chairman, no doubt well versed in this part of Jewish history, couldn't dissociate the name Shulman from the name Boruch. What made me even more resentful was that the audience, during the question period, also addressed me as "Genosse Boruch Shulman."

At the end of the lecture, a small, fragile woman got up and suggested that the audience express their heartiest thanks to our "Genosse Boruch Shulman for his stimulating talk." The audience clapped again and the chairman presented the motion to the gathering. "Who is for expressing our heartiest thanks to Genosse Boruch Shulman?" The audience rose like one man and this time the applause was accompanied by the stamping of feet. "Come again, Boruch Shulman," a tall man with a hearing aid shouted at me as I departed for home.

I realized later how lucky I had been to have only my first name changed. Since then, another chairman introduced me as Mr. Ephraim Shulsinger. The name gave me no cue to get up and I remained in my seat. The chairman turned toward me, gave me a surprised look, kicked me softly in the ankle, and asked: "Mr. Shulsinger, you fell asleep?" I got up slowly and walked over the lectern. I looked at the audience and they looked back at me. I didn't feel hurt. After all, what difference did it make whether they looked at Shulman or Shulsinger? I was gratified that at least both Shulman and Shulsinger had the first syllable in common. But I defy psychoanalysts to find the link between Shulman and Kamenetzki.

On another occasion the chairman was thin, dark and had a mustache that made him resemble Ferdinand Lassalle. He wasn't very communicative and hardly exchanged a word with the officers around the table. He gave me a cool, furtive look when I was presented to him by the secretary. He was evidently feared by the audience, for when he got up everybody froze in his seat. Then he announced that he was "presenting the guest speaker of the evening, Mr. Kamenetzki." I threw an astonished glance at the secretary, who smiled, waved his hand, and motioned me toward the microphone, After I finished, the chairman declared that, "Now Mr. Kamenetzki will answer questions from the audience," and finished off the evening with a brief, "Thank you, Mr. Kamenetzki."

Terrible? Not at all. At least he stuck to the name

Kamenetzki with faithful consistency, unlike another chairman who introduced me as "our friend Strapman," then called me "Mr. Schwartzman" during the question period, and concluded the evening with the words: "I hope that you have all enjoyed the lecture of Mr. Stollman." A few days later, I received a check made out to Mr. Schmaltzman.

For some time I accepted all this with surprising stoicism. But as time passed, the stoicism began to wane. A feeling of silent revolt was beginning to take possession of me. It developed slowly, until it finally burst into the open during a lecture in Brooklyn where I was invited to talk on the "Golem" of H. Leivick. The chairman was a soft-spoken man, the very personification of gentleness. From the moment of my arrival at the hall, he took me under his wing. He personally hung up my hat and coat, brought me a glass of water, and set the microphone at the proper height. He was my guardian and my protector. Only when it came to the official act of introducing me, he said briefly, "Ladies and Gentlemen, I give you Mr. Abraham Milman." Phonetically, Milman had much more in common with Shulman than Kamenetzki or even Shulsinger, but it was perhaps due to his gentleness that I felt a wave of rage. Instead of getting up, I remained in my seat and hissed like a rattlesnake: "I am not Milman." He looked at me in a friendly way, smiled apologetically, nodded and made a quick correction: "Ladies and Gentlemen, the speaker has just drawn it to my attention that his name is NOT Milman." He then reached out and helped me over to the mike. To this day the audience doesn't know who the speaker was—except that it was NOT Milman. It should be pointed out that some of the chairmen are well aware of these risks, and have developed an efficient method of avoiding them.

It is such a simple solution that I am amazed it hasn't

been adopted as a general rule. Many chairmen simply don't disclose the name of the speaker at all. They say only: "It is my privilege to present to you the speaker of the evening." Period. No first name, no last name—nothing. Some go even further and save themselves the trouble of memorizing the title of the lecture: "It is with great satisfaction that I present the speaker who will speak on the subject written in the invitation." Thus the chairman has skillfully avoided both the Scylla of name and the Charybdis of subject. And what's more—an introduction like this can be used perennially.

Only once did a chairman change my very gender. He introduced me as "Mrs. Shulman." The program that evening consisted of two parts. The first half was devoted to my lecture on Jewish literature. The second half, following an intermission during which the public was treated to coffee and cake, was to be devoted to folk songs. It was justly assumed that the audience, after listening for an hour to a lecturer, deserved a reward in the form of songs. The singer on this occasion was an elderly lady in an evening dress of purple taffeta, with a pince-nez resting on her chest. For some reason, the chairman felt that it was the lady who was to give the lecture, while the younger man in the black suit and polka dot tie, was the coloratura singer. He waited patiently until the audience quieted down. He then looked sharply at the lady and announced that "It is with particular pleasure that I give the floor to Mrs. Shulman." The lady didn't budge and he tried to help her up. She gave him a frightened look and clung to her chair with both hands. Convinced that she was hard of hearing, the chairman shouted into her ear: "Mrs. Shulman, you have the floor." She flushed and began mumbling something which the chairman took for a fit of stage fright. He now tried to get her up by force, grabbing hold of her elbow. I decided to put an end to the confusion and started briskly for the mike. He caught me by a sleeve and hissed: "Go back to your seat, you will sing later." I freed myself from his grip and began the lecture with the remarks: "My friends, I wish to make a clinical correction." Nobody even chuckled and I continued with the first line of the lecture that "Jewish literature more than any other has a social awareness."

WHO IS THAT GUY?

The members of a Jewish Community Center west of the Hudson invited me to lecture on the subject: "The destruction of European Jewry as depicted in the literature of other nations." The bus connection was good—there was a bus leaving every fifteen minutes. Once inside, I had enough time to review the main points of the lecture.

The secretary was waiting at the station. We had never met before, but we recognized each other right away. He drove me in his car, but the distance was too short to exchange more than a few casual remarks. We arrived at the front of the Community Center and I was pleasantly impressed. The building was large, with two huge marble candelabras on each side of the stairs; the windows were high and brightly lit. Inside, the hall was flooded with light from crystal chandeliers, and long tables covered with sparkling white cloths held big vases with flowers. All the men were in black suits or tuxedos and the ladies wore the most stylish dresses.

As soon as I entered, accompanied by the secretary, the chairman of the evening, wearing a tuxedo, rose from his seat and walked toward me with outstretched arms. He led me to the Table of Honor. He, himself, sat on my right, and a young rabbi wearing a white and blue yarmulka, sat on my left.

I was delighted and also puzzled, for in the middle of our table stood a massive silver plate with a big tiered cake bearing a forest of candles. I suddenly had a dark premonition and whispered to the chairman:

—What is this?

—What is what?

—There. On the plate.

—You mean the cake?

—Yes.

—It's a cake.

—Is it the custom of your organization to feed the speaker with cakes?

—The cake, he said, is not for the speaker. It's for the president of our Center.

—And why the candles?

The chairman looked surprised: "Why not? Don't they put up candles to celebrate golden wedding anniversaries where you come from?"

Only now did I comprehend the chandeliers, the flowers, the tuxedos and the ladies' evening gowns.

"How come," said I to the chairman in a weak voice, "you have added a wedding anniversary to my lecture?"

"We didn't," he said, "add the wedding anniversary to your lecture. We added your lecture to the anniversary. Our executive thought it would be nice to embellish the occasion of our president's wedding anniversary with a bit of culture."

Just then a tremendous commotion broke out at the door. The whole audience sprang to their feet and began to applaud. Through the widely opened door came the president, a tiny man in a top hat, and his wife, a microscopic woman bedecked with pearls and diamonds. Both walked triumphantly, nodding to the right and left, while the audience broke out with a loud "For he's a jolly good fellow." The elderly couple floated on a wave of enthusiasm toward the table where they were seated in front of the cake. The chairman managed to quell the noise of the gathering and suggested that we all join him in singing the well-known Yiddish song: "Eighty-he, and seventy-she." The public obliged and continued with another song: "Oy, Avram, I cannot live without you" (the name of the president was Abraham Aybeshitz). This was followed with "Hot a Yid a Waybele," and "Rumania, Rumania," although both the president and his wife originally came from Russia.

I was the only one who didn't join the singing. I was squeezed in between the chairman and the rabbi and furtively looked into my notes which contained the general points of my lecture: "The Destruction of European Jewry." I came upon a quotation from John Hersey's book: "The Wall" just when the president began to blow out the fifty candles, which he managed to do to the joy of the gathering. Then the chairman turned to me and in a very elegant manner handed me a huge knife. It was to be my honor to cut the cake. I did it clumsily. The chairman then gave the floor to the president himself. The enthusiasm of the audience was indescribable. The tiny president paid tribute to his deceased parents. His father "olov hasholem," he said, had been a soldier in the army of Czar Alexander the First, and his mother, "olov hasholem," could play the piano and was addressed as "Mademoiselle." He related the circumstances of their betrothal, and of the marriage, and he was by no means a dull speaker. He embellished his talk with spicy jokes on subjects such as wedding nights, virginity and virility. The public roared with laughter.

The president finally finished and sat back in a cloud of admiration. Then the public drank a noisy toast. After which the chairman rose and announced that he was giving the floor to the guest speaker of the evening. The audience responded with outstretched glasses and sang "For he's a jolly good fellow." When the song died down, I pulled out my notes and began to read the title of my lecture.

I saw the president turn toward the chairman and, nodding in my direction, ask in a shrill voice: "Who is that guy?"

A SHREWD CHAIRMAN

The subject of the lecture was: "Our national poet—Ye-huda Halevi." The advertisement said 8 P.M. and I arrived a few minutes early. Nobody was there. At a quarter to nine the chairman appeared and asked me cheerfully: "What chased you out of your house?"

The people slowly gathered; at 9:30 the chairman banged on the table with a wooden gavel, and announced that he was now opening the annual general meeting of the "branch." He added that as soon as the meeting was over "our esteemed Genosse Shulman" will give a lecture. He motioned me to come up to the podium where he offered me one of the principal chairs around the table. He courteously waited for me to sit down and said: "My friends, it's my pleasure to welcome our distinguished guest." To which he added a phrase which puzzled me: "As you all know, Genosse Shulman is a widely read satirical writer with a poisonous pen." I was thinking: "Why the hell did he have to say that?"

It was clear from the very beginning that the annual meeting was going to be stormy. As soon as the secretary finished reading the report of the committee's activities during the preceding year, there were loud shouts from the members of the audience: "It's a lie! It's a fabrication! It's a forgery!"

Several people jumped up from their seats and began

shouting. At this moment the chairman slowly rose to his feet, hit the table with the gavel and said quietly: "My friends, I've already told you that there's a stranger in our midst and it would be most inappropriate to wash our dirty linen in the presence of such a distinguished guest."

I suddenly understood why he had so generously invited me to sit in the center of the praesidium.

The proceedings included a debate and the chairman gave the floor to a young fellow with a cluster of yellow hair. The chairman suggested that the man should speak from his place, but the yellow-headed fellow ran forward to the front of the platform. Here he began shouting:

"Enough. We shall no longer let ourselves be led by our noses by this gang of shlemiels and good-for-nothings. For the entire year they didn't put a finger in cold water and now they have the chutspah to appear before the general meeting and expect us to elect them again. Never! Never! Never!"

The chairman said to him sweetly: "Genosse Mlynek, may I ask you to be a little more careful with your choice of words. We mustn't forget that we have among us a man who is quite capable of besmearing us in his newspaper."

Genosse Mlynek who was on the verge of exploding in a new venomous tirade, gave me a dirty look and hurriedly returned to his seat. A tall member with a small quadrangular mustache stepped forward. He galloped to the mike and started pulling scribbled notes out of his pockets. He brought one of them to his eyes and began to read: "I hereby state categorically that the secretary's report was a swindle and a heap of falsehoods. I appeal to all the friends present to take the executive members by their heads and throw them down the stairs."

The chairman stopped him: "Comrade Silbershatz, I'll kindly ask you to reserve your gutter language for another occasion. We have among us a celebrated writer and it is our duty, now more than ever, to behave like civilized human beings."

Comrade Silberhatz collected his notes and went back to his seat. The same thing happened with the next two. The first one said only that he came to tonight's meeting with the intention of giving the committee members "bloody hell" but due to the presence of the stranger he would put it off till some other time. The second was a woman. She wore great earrings the size of frying pans. All she said was "What a pity that we have such a distinguished guest."

During all this time I'd been sitting on hot coals. So this was the executive's aim. They needed the lecture like a hole in the head. All they wanted was to plant me here as a gendarme to scare the members away from opening their mouths. However a new development threatened to undermine the committee's strategy. A white-haired man with a silver pince-nez got up and said: "We all agree with the chairman that we can't openly say what we think about the idiots of the executive in front of our distinguished guest. I therefore suggest that our esteemed visitor kindly leave this room for the duration of the meeting."

The proposal was greeted with thunderous applause. The chairman had no choice but to put the motion to a vote. An overwhelming majority was in favor of the suggestion that I get the hell out of the room.

"Alright," said the confounded chairman, "the majority has expressed its desire that our guest leave the room. But where, may I ask, should he go? We can't let him walk in the street in such weather. It's raining."

"Let's lend him an umbrella," suggested the lady with the gigantic earrings. Several members came running with umbrellas. But I was saved at the moment by a gentle little lady who wore a hearing aid: "Friends," she said, "we can't let him walk the streets at this late hour. He may, God forbid, be attacked by some mugger."

The man with the quadrangular mustache came out with a practical suggestion: "He can leave his wallet and watch with the treasurer." But the very mention of the word "mugger" had a calming effect on the most excitable minds. To carry on a fight against the imbeciles of the executive was one thing, but to pay for this with the blood of an invited speaker was unacceptable even to the man with the cluster of yellow hair. So the chairman continued the meeting with me sitting all the time like a member of the National Guard. And when one of the members, planted by the committee, suggested that the same committee remain in office another year, nobody protested.

When I finally got up to talk about "Our national poet—Yehuda Halevi," I noticed that all the members of the committee had disappeared. They'll no doubt come back next year with another invited speaker who will play, as I did this night, the role of a scarecrow.

A HEALTH RESTAURANT IN KANSAS CITY

The function of a lecturer is to provide the audience with spiritual food, and it often happens that the audience repays the lecturer with a kind of food that is more palpable. The lecture over, there is usually among the audience one who would invite the speaker to a local restaurant. As a rule the desire is not solely to perform an act of hospitality; their real motive is to boast of the specialties of their regional cuisine.

In the course of my career as a roving lecturer I was treated to such gourmet masterpieces in most of the American and Canadian states; from the Indian dishes in the eating places in Saskatchewan in the North to the French "cordon bleu" in New Orleans restaurants in the South. I soon learned to pick from the menus a dish that contained both nourishing ingredients as well as romantic elements of the local folklore.

I could, did I have the wisdom I possess now, write an account of all these culinary expeditions and have another book ready, a supplement to this one, named: "The Adventures of an Eating Lecturer." But not all adventures would be of a cheerful nature. One of them was quite a disaster. The catastrophic incident took place in Kansas City, in the state of Missouri.

The subject of my lecture was the perennial theme: "The Three Yiddish Classics." It ended, including the traditional question time, at eight in the evening. People of the audience began crowding around the platform supplementing their former applause with additional handshakes and compliments. A tiny elderly man with a white butterfly-shaped moustache waited at the door and when I was about to leave approached me timidly and said in a soft voice,

"I liked your lecture."

"Thank you."

"I'm also a reader and admirer of your articles."

"Thank you."

"I assume that you are now ready to return to your hotel."

"Indeed, I am."

"I wonder if you'd do me the honor and have supper with me."

The idea of having supper in a place charged with such romantic names as Kansas and Missouri appealed to me immensely.

On the way to the restaurant, a few blocks away from the lecture hall, my new friend presented himself as one of the eldest Jewish inhabitants in this part of the South; he also spoke of his old and unshakable attachment to the Three Yiddish Classics who were the subject of my tonight's lecture. We had in the meantime passed a few restaurants and steak houses, but each time the elderly man would wave them aside with his small hand saying we were not going into any of these places where the foodstuff served was "adulterated by human hands." His words sounded cryptical and I was growing curious.

With another block behind us he turned into a little street and stopped in front of a place which had a large sign printed in purple: "Walk in and eat in health." Inside, the place was crowded with small wooden tables scattered chaotically over the floor. The four walls of this unusual looking place were hung with huge posters carrying strange messages. One of them said in capital letters: "Don't bite your food—chew it." Each poster was supplied by a timetable explaining how long one ought to chew the various foods: wheat grains—three minutes; the skin of horseradishes—two minutes; roots of chestnut trees—four minutes. And so forth.

I looked askingly at my new friend and my friend looked cheerfully back: "This is the only place in the whole South, if not in the whole United States of America, where they serve you none of the disease-infected poisons."

We settled at one of the tables in the center of the room. My immediate neighbor at my right was a lady with her hair pulled back into a bun. She was thin and emaciated and looked like a sack of loosely packed bones. Before her was a plate of oats. She kept her mouth shut, moving her jaws like a horse.

"What is she doing?" I asked.

"She is chewing her oats," replied my friend.

A waiter came over, and when I looked at him I wanted to scream "Shema Yisroel!" a scream pious Jews let out when they encounter a ghost. Actually, the waiter looked less like a ghost than a corpse who had crawled out from the bottom of a family grave. He handed us a grey sheet of cardboard with imprinted dishes, each of the dishes marked by two figures: on the left was the price, and on the right, the number of minutes it should be chewed.

My friend selected a plate of pine tree cones and advised me to try the sawdust of mulberry wood. "Eat it," he said, "you will not find any such sawdust in all the United States."

At that moment the door opened and in walked a family of four: a father, a mother and two youngsters. The father looked like a tall, black unopened umbrella, the mother resembled a broomstick dressed in a pink skirt, and the two young fellows were taken directly from a horror film which specializes in transparent nightmares. The couple noticed my friend and they exchanged greetings. I asked who they were and my friend obliged: the man was the author of a best-selling book in Missouri, "How to Eat to Be Powerful;" the woman was a popular preacher in the South, where she talked on the "Advantages of Eating the Leaves of Needle Trees." "What about the kids? Have they been brought from Calcutta?" My friend didn't notice the irony and replied: "No, they look the way they do because they have only recently started coming to this restaurant."

The waiter brought them plates filled with a greenish liquid. "What is it they ordered?" I asked. My friend couldn't reply, for he was in the process of chewing a pine tree cone (four minutes). I took a spoon of my own sawdust and tried to swallow it, but instead I began to choke. My friend pointed to the chart on the wall, where it said that mulberry sawdust should not be swallowed but chewed (three minutes). I took another mouthful of sawdust and began chewing, which gave me the opportunity of looking around.

My neighbor on my left was a man with a bony face and an enormous Adam's apple. He wore a black sweater and I was sure that behind the sweater he had a case of naked ribs. His partner was a woman. When I looked at her, she had just opened her navy blue lips and put inside a spoonful of oak leaves. I managed to see that her teeth were the same color as the leaves.

The waiter again came by on his two dead feet and brought us dessert: young branches of acacia shrubs. My friend snatched one of them and began chewing it. He looked at me in puzzlement for I didn't touch the acacia, but he couldn't talk before the five minutes of chewing the acacia branch were over. He then asked:

"What's the matter? Why aren't you eating?"

"I'm no longer hungry. I ate a lot of the mulberry sawdust."

"Would you like a dessert? They have delicious willow leaves dipped in eucalyptus oil."

"No, thanks, I never overeat before I go to sleep."

He accompanied me later to my hotel. Before saying good night he gave me a small card. "This is the address of the restaurant, in case you ever come back to Missouri." We shook hands and I walked into the lobby of the hotel. As soon as my charming benefactor was out of sight, I turned around, ran hurriedly out of the hotel, and jumped into the first restaurant across the street. There I sat at the nearest table and when a full-bosomed young waitress with a face as white as milk, asked me what I wished, I said: "A roasted chicken."

"A quarter or a half?"

"Make it the biggest rooster you have in the kitchen." I later plunged all my thirty-two teeth in the soft meat of the bird.

FEODOR DOSTOYEVSKY AND SHALOM ALEYKHEM

Despite all the publicity and mailed invitations, the hall where I was to give my lecture was empty. The chairman was there, the secretary was there, and so was the treasurer who had set up a little table at the door to collect the entrance fee—but there was almost nobody to collect from. It was neither too hot nor too cold, nor was it raining or snowing. So the weather was no excuse. Was it the subject? I was to lecture on "Feodor Mikhaylovitch Dostoyevsky— his life and works," and I knew from previous experience that this always draws a crowd. But whatever the reason, the hall was practically empty and the room looked like the epilogue of Ionesco's play "The Chairs." This was all I could see from my honorary seat in the praesidium—a sea of chairs.

When it became evident that nobody else would arrive, the chairman told the treasurer to fold up his improvised ticket office; he then signaled me to get up to the mike and start delivering the speech. I got up and faced the chairs that had been prepared for the public with such loving care. But the public consisted of half a dozen men and women who sat crowded together like abandoned sheep.

The secretary shared my feeling of dejection. Before I opened my lips, I heard him say to the chairman:

—Mr. Tsimring, there's another person in the building, Mrs. Zaydenbaytel. Shall I tell her to come in?

—Where is she?—asked the chairman.

—In the library. I saw her there before I came in. Shall I go and fetch her?

The chairman's voice was soaked in irony: "You ask if you should? Go there this minute and bring her in." And to me he said: "Let's wait another moment till Mrs. Zaydenbaytel comes."

The secretary sprightly left the room, but a minute later came back alone.

—She doesn't want to come—he reported.

—Doesn't want—what?

—To come.

—Why not?

—She's in the middle of a book.

The chairman banged on the table: "Did you tell her that we're having a lecture?"

—Yes.

—And?

—She wouldn't budge.

The chairman's voice became harsh: "You told her the subject of the lecture?"

—Feodor Mikhaylovitch Dostoyevsky—his life and works. I also told her the name of the lecturer.

—And what was her reaction?

—Her reaction was nothing. She wants to stay where she is.

The chairman, Mr. Tsimring, who despite his white hair had a pitch-black moustache, banged on the table again: "What book is she reading?"

—Collected stories of Shalom Aleykhem.

—Go and tell her that she can read the book after the

lecture is over. She can take the book home. Or we can give her the book as a present. Right now she must fulfill her duties as a member and take part in our cultural activities.

Again, the secretary got up and left the room, which gave me another chance to go through the thesis of my lecture. A minute passed, the door opened and the secretary was back. Alone. Without Mrs. Zaydenbaytel.

—Nu?—asked the chairman.

—Nu-nu, replied the secretary.

—She isn't coming?

—No.

—Why?

—She wants to read.

—Did you tell her that we're all waiting?

—You can't argue with Mrs. Zaydenbaytel. She's an obstinate woman.

—Maybe it's because of the dollar that we charge?

—I told her that we'd let her in free.

—And?

—And nothing.

The chairman turned to the treasurer: "Mr. Baygelman, you shall go with the secretary and help him bring Mrs. Zaydenbaytel. Don't come back without her."

He said it in a menacing voice. The two gentlemen got up and left the room. This gave me another opportunity to run through my notes about Dostoyevsky.

Two minutes later the door opened with a loud bang. Mrs. Zaydenbaytel, a massive woman, was brought in by the secretary and the treasurer, both tightly holding on to her elbows. Together they looked like the two gangsters and Herr K. from the final scene in Kafka's "The Trial." Mrs. Zaydenbaytel was carrying a large book and as soon as she was dragged by her escorts to the nearest chair, she opened the book and began to read.

The chairman turned towards me: "Mr. Shulman, you may begin."

I did. But it appeared that this wasn't the end of my predicament. For while I was talking on the life and works of Feodor Mikhaylovitch, Mrs. Zaydenbaytel was reading her book and every few seconds burst out in gales of laughter. Once she must have come to a particularly funny paragraph, for she began roaring like a gorilla.

This was too much for the chairman. He gave me a sign to stop and addressed the lady: "Mrs. Zaydenbaytel," he said, "you may, if you so wish, go ahead with your reading, but for God's sake, you must stop this laughter."

"Impossible," replied Mrs. Zaydenbaytel, "you simply can't read Shalom Aleykhem and keep your mouth shut."

I was in the middle of telling the story of "Crime and Punishment," describing how the student Raskolnikoff was murdering with his ax the old Alevna Ivanovna. I closed my eyes a moment and had a terrible vision: it was not Raskolnikoff but myself who was chopping off the head of Mrs. Zaydenbaytel.

A VERY STRANGE BEHAVIOR

All the chairs were occupied. The crowd was in an excellent mood, friendly and cheerful. The "Stimmung" was responsive. When the chairman got up and asked everyone to take their seat, the listeners responded with a hilarious applause. They clapped when the secretary read the minutes of the previous meeting. They cheered when the treasurer called on the members to pay the outstanding dues. A veritable storm erupted when another committee member announced that the branch was organizing an excursion to Washington. The clapping was so enthusiastic that he had to encore the announcement and then he was allowed to sit down in another outburst of acclaim.

But all this behavior came to an end when I walked over to the lectern and began delivering my speech. I spoke for three quarters of an hour—I interspersed the talk with puns, paradoxes, anecdotes and outright jokes—all this was of no use. They sat like clay statues. Even after I finished and walked back to my seat, there was a complete and total silence.

But as soon as the chairman rose from his chair and announced that now the Ladies Group will serve tea with cheesecake, there was again stormy applause. The applause turned into a tornado when the chairman presented the lady who baked the cake. The clapping was so contagious that I myself sprang to my feet clapping and shouting "bravo."

A WOMAN NAMED DEVOYRA

It was cold in New York but nothing compared to the frost in Montreal. I wasn't properly dressed and shivered all the way from the airport to the hotel and, later, from the hotel to the meeting hall.

As I opened the door to the lobby, a short man in a checkered sports jacket looked at me and exclaimed: "What a surprise!" He shot out his arms. I did the same. We fell into each others grasp and kissed in the French fashion on both cheeks.

He was short and plump with greyish temples and a shiny bald spot in the middle of his head. We disentangled, looked at each other with love and embraced for a second time. I didn't know exactly who he was, but judging from this riotous encounter he must have been one of the closest human beings in the history of my life.

There was still some time before the lecture and he suggested that we go to the canteen in the building. We went down the stairs, holding hands, and sat at a small table. A waiter brought us coffee and cheese cakes. The man in the sports jacket looked at me with rapture and I looked back with enchantment. He said joyously: "After all this time." I said: "At last." He started the idiom:

"Mountains never meet . . ." I finished it: "but humans do." He gazed at me with happiness and I gazed back with fascination, wondering at the same time: "Who the hell is he?"

Judging from our embrace and his outburst of love he must have been a most intimate friend. I tried to classify him geographically. Where had we met? In which part of the world? It had to be a place I had stayed long enough to develop a friendship of such magnitude. Was it Poland, Australia, France or Israel? I quoted a Polish poet: "Litwo, ojczyzno moja . . ." He gave me a bewildered look. He reacted in the same way when I said: "How are the kangaroos in Melbourne?" to "Comment ça va, mon vieux?" and "Ma shlomcha, chabibi?" Was it in South America? I suddenly exclaimed with no reason whatsoever: "Mucho gusto, hasta luego" and "How's the cruzeiro?" He pretended to concentrate on the cheesecake, but I could see that he, too, was beginning to have his doubts. The simplest thing was to ask: "Who the devil are you?" but this, after such an embrace, was out of the question. My mind was working feverishly: had we met in Iran? In Hong Kong? In Ceylon? Casablanca? The coffee was bad, the cake was sour, the atmosphere around the table became intolerable. I was tempted to use my sense of humor and say cheerfully: "We've stepped into quite a mess, haven't we?" But my sense of humor had vanished. I suddenly had a brilliant idea. I looked into his eyes and asked:

"How is Devoyra?"

My idea was this: he'll say: "Who's Devoyra?" To which I'll respond: "Your wife's name is not Devoyra? I thought you were Devoyra's husband." I'll then gracefully apologize and walk away. But something unexpected happened. As soon as I asked: "How is Devoyra?" he answered: "Devoyra had an operation."

The situation was no longer tragic, it was a catastrophe.

Of all possible names, like a blind horse I had picked the name of his wife! Now there was no way back.

—What sort of operation?

—Kidney.

—Which kidney, the left or the right?

—The right.

—What do the doctors say?

—They don't know yet.

—When will they know?

—In another week.

—Is she back home?

—Who?

—Devoyra.

—Where else should she be?

—Is she under medical care?

—What do you mean?

—Does she have a nurse?

—Who?

—Devoyra.

I knew that the best thing was to keep my mouth shut. But some devil pushed me:

—One should be careful with kidneys.

—One should be careful with everything—he said.

—Particularly with kidneys—I said.

—Why particularly?

—There are no more than two of them.

He swallowed a piece of cake. I added:

—On the other hand, it's better to have sick kidneys than a sick heart.

—Why's that?

—There's only one heart.

He gulped his coffee and began coughing. I said:

—I had a cousin who had trouble with his kidneys all his life.

—Oh, yes?

—Yes. But it's funny that in the end he didn't die because of his kidneys.

—No?

—No. He fell out of a window.

—Very funny.

—Another cousin also suffered from his kidneys.

—Is that so?

—But the doctors operated on his bladder.

—Why?

—They made a mistake.

His eyes, which were blue, became as dark as pitch. I said:

—My uncle's first born child had three kidneys.

The situation became terrible. I bit my tongue, but I couldn't hold myself back.

—They say that Napoleon Bonaparte fell a victim to his kidneys.

—Oh, yes?

—But not Alexander the Great.

The man was as pale as a sheet. He started playing with his knife and I expected that one more phrase from me and he would plunge it into my kidneys. But a miracle occurred. The door opened and a man came up to my table.

"Genosse Shulman," he said, "it's time to start."

I got up. So did the man. Without a word, we both shot out our arms and embraced again. Before leaving I said to him: "Give my regards to Devoyra."

Later, as I rose to speak, I looked for the man whose wife's name was Devoyra. When I saw that he wasn't there I spoke with more gusto than ever.

A VOTE OF THANKS

After I concluded my talk: "Yiddish literature between the two World Wars," the chairman of the cultural afternoon did an unusual thing. He said that he wasn't going to thank the speaker in the name of the audience, rather he wanted the audience to express its own gratitude and admiration. He therefore introduced a "motion of thanks for the spiritual joy we have derived from the lecture." The motion was seconded by the vice-chairman who added the adjective "intellectual." This finally was extended still further by the secretary who threw in another adjective "Jewish;" so that I was thanked for the "spiritual, intellectual and Jewish joy."

The motion was carried unanimously.

All this took place in a city in Michigan. When everything was over I shook hands with the members of the board, said good-bye to the audience and left the hall. I went in the company of a friend who I once knew in Europe and who now lived in this city. It was a pleasant day, my plane back to New York was to leave later in the evening and there was ample time for a stroll along the shores of the lake and through the quiet streets of the town. We walked until my friend brought me to a kosher deli.

We sat at a table and were approached by an elderly, ginger-headed waiter wearing a yarmulka. There was no need to read the menu, there were red stains of borsht on

45

his apron and we ordered two borshts with mashed potatoes. The waiter asked: "Gravy?" We looked again, saw signs of delicious gravy on his apron and said "Yes."

Two minutes later he brought our plates with royal purple borsht and pyramids of snow white potatoes soaked in a golden sauce. It smelled and tasted wonderful.

After the soup we ordered the "spécialité de la maison"—kreplach with minced meat. But as soon as I plunged my fork into one of the kreplach, the door of the restaurant opened and in came three men, the ruling triumvirate of the organization where I had given my talk: the chairman (who had formulated the "vote of thanks" with the adjective "spiritual"); his vice-chairman (who had added "intellectual"), and the secretary (who had rounded it up with the obscure "Jewish"). The trio, without seeing the presence of their speaker, occupied a table directly behind my back. I preferred to remain incognito and enjoy the company of my friend who I hadn't seen for so many years. I heard the chairman (who had a rich and vibrating voice) order a rossel-soup. The vice-chairman who spoke in a thin soprano wanted a "shtchav" and the secretary, whose voice was flat and dry, opted for a "cabbage soup with a bone."

After ordering they began a loud conversation to which I paid no attention for I was engaged in my own with my friend. But suddenly I caught a word that put me in a state of alert. I heard the chairman say "lecture." He pronounced it in a way which caused his two companions to giggle. I pretended to listen to what my friend was telling me, but I was paying very close attention to what was happening at the table immediately behind me.

I heard the thin voice of the vice-chairman: "He's a nudnik." This was corrected by the dry voice of the secretary: "He's not a nudnik, he's a cludnik" (which—in the lingo of these people—meant: classical nudnik). The chairman suggested a compromise: "Gentlemen, let's agree on hudnik," (the letter "h" stands for "horrible").

This was followed by another exchange of brief epigrams. The chairman said: "He killed the lecture." The vice-chairman corrected: "He assassinated it." The secretary improved still further: "He slaughtered it."

My friend, who was sitting opposite me couldn't hear any of these words, but could see my face. I tried in vain to pick up a krepel with the fork, but my hand was trembling and the krepel kept slipping back.

—What's the matter?—my friend asked.

—Nothing—I said.

—You've suddenly become pale.

—I'm alright.

—You're as white as a corpse.

—I'm fine.

—Didn't you like the borsht?

—The borsht was delicious.

—Anything wrong with the kreplach?

—The kreplach are divine.

To divert his suspicion I swallowed a whole krepel and almost choked. I sat back to hear more. What I heard made me shudder.

The chairman said: "He butchered Shalom Ash." The vice-chairman said: "He garroted Zalmen Schneur." The secretary said: "He asphyxiated Abraham Raisin." The chairman said: "He immolated H. Leywick." The vice-chairman said: "He decapitated Moyshe Leyb Halperin." The secretary concluded: "He smothered Itzik Manger."

I attempted to pierce another krepel with the fork, but the fork hit the plate. My friend got hold of my arm.

—Don't eat any more. You're sick.

—I'm not.

—You're yellow as a lemon.

—It's the light.

—I'll order a glass of alka-seltzer.

—It's not necessary.

—Stop eating the kreplach.

—I love kreplach.

To prove it I swallowed another one, choked and again leaned back. I was in time to catch a whole phrase of the chairman who quoted a Yiddish saying: "What was good wasn't his, what was his wasn't good." "Yes," said the vice-chairman. "He's a pain in the neck." "In the ass," corrected the secretary. And the trio burst out with a healthy laughter. The chairman returned to his brief epigrams: "It wasn't a lecture, it was a massacre." "A carnage," said his vice. The secretary improved: "A pogrom."

"Let's go," said my friend who was watching me all this time with frightened eyes. "You must get some fresh air."

He called the waiter and asked for the check. I saw signs of my favorite dessert on the waiter's apron: strawberries. But my friend had already gotten up. I also rose, turned around and met the chairman's eyes.

"Look who is here," he exclaimed. "Our distinguished guest speaker."

He extended an arm and shook my hand. His two companions sprang to their feet and invited me to join them, but my friend explained that I wasn't feeling well and he was taking me for a walk.

The chairman said: "Thank you again for the spiritual joy."

"Spiritual and intellectual," added the vice-chairman.

I looked at the secretary. He took the cue: "And Jewish." He looked at me with gratitude and admiration.

PAYING RESPECTS

Paying respects to "members who have passed away" is part of every Yiddish cultural gathering. The procedure is as solemn as it is simple.

The chairman has before him a list of those who have died since the last meeting and it is his sad duty to ask the audience to rise and remain standing until he finishes reading the list. Very often the list of the deceased is supplemented by a recital of the names of the members who are at the time of the meeting incapacitated by sickness. When this occurs, the chairman, in the name of all present, sends every one of them wishes for a "full recovery." The wishes for recovery are usually followed by applause.

But once I witnessed an instance when the formal act of paying respects and sending wishes for recovery caused a serious disturbance.

The lecture started at half past eight. It appeared from the introductory words of the chairman that this was the first cultural gathering of the year that required the two usual obligations: paying tribute to members who had passed away and sending the proper wishes to the others who were sick.

"Friends," he said, "before proceeding with the agenda, I'll ask all those gathered to rise and pay tribute to the memory of those of our members who have left us during the last year." The audience, like a troop of disciplined soldiers, rose and stood with bowed heads while the chairman read from a black-rimmed sheet of paper the names of the deceased:

"Friend Solomon Belken . . . Friend Fishel Hochstein . . . Friend Sarah Faysh . . . Friend Berel Zylberman . . ."

At the mention of Berel Zylberman, one of the men at the praesidium table ostentatiously sat down. The chairman looked at him with surprise. "Genosse Baygelman! I am not finished with the list. We are still in the act of paying tribute to the memories of our departed."

Genosse Baygelman looked at him defiantly. "I have no intention of paying respect to the memory of Berel Zylberman."

"Why not?"

"Because he didn't pay his membership dues. He was three years behind."

"Genosse Baygelman," the chairman said with a threatening look, "this is hardly the time for collecting dues. Our friend Berel Zylberman was a member of our organization and he passed away. It is our duty to get up and honor his memory."

"You can all stand there till next Purim and give all the honors to the memory of Berel Zylberman. But as far as I am concerned, I am going to sit down."

The chairman began to lose his temper.

"Baygelman!" he said, "either you get up and pay tribute or I'll move at the next meeting of the executive to have you replaced as treasurer."

Baygelman sat unmoved for another minute, but he finally changed his mind. It was clear that he was affected by the threat of being expelled from the executive, and that put an end to his revolt. He got up, very slowly, and said so that everybody in the room could hear:

"I'm doing it out of a sense of discipline. It has no connection with Berel Zylberman."

It was probably this act of rebellion on the part of the treasurer that encouraged another man, this time an ordinary member of the organization, to stage another demonstration, this time on a smaller scale. After the audience had returned to their seats, the chairman pulled another list from his pocket. "I'll now read the names of our members who couldn't participate in tonight's cultural event because they are either in hospitals or sick in their homes. I suggest that we send every one of them our wishes for a speedy recovery." Again he began to recite in a gloomy voice:

"We wish a speedy recovery to our member Benjamin Kukla . . . Zlata Sosha . . . Yosel Blank . . ."

"I'm against it," a voice suddenly sounded from the audience. A small man with a white goatee jumped up from his seat and explained:

"Yosel Blank is as healthy as a horse. There is no need to send him wishes for recovery."

"How can you say such a thing," the chairman reprimanded him, "last week he had a heart attack."

"I wish all Jews to have heart attacks like he had," said the short fellow with the goatee. "He is healthier than you and I."

"So why is he in bed?"

"He is in bed because he is as lazy as a turtle. He wants his wife to wait on him like a slave."

The chairman, who obviously had his own doubts about Joseph Blank, suggested a compromise.

"Suppose," he said, "he didn't have a real heart attack, that it was actually, as you suggested, an excuse to have his wife wait on him. What wrong can it do to send him our wishes for a speedy recovery?"

"Because," said the man, "a speedy recovery would be

to him not a blessing but a catastrophe. He would have to get up from bed and start working."

The chairman reflected for a second and decided on a democratic procedure—to hand the matter over to the assembled members.

"Who is for sending wishes for recovery to our Genosse Yosel Blank?"

Only a few people raised their hands.

"Who is against it?"

This time more than half the audience shot up their arms.

"The motion to send Yosel Blank wishes for a speedy recovery is withdrawn."

There was enthusiastic applause. After it died down I got up and announced the name of the lecture: "The Wise Men of Chelm."

THE LIVING
AND THE DEAD

A small town in Texas. I arrived by bus from another part of the state and a taxi brought me to an exotic hotel, the front of which looked like the façade of a two dimensional saloon in a Western film. An hour later I had an unexpected visit from an elderly gentleman. He was the oldest Jewish inhabitant of this town and he told me that it was his perennial mission to look after the "cultural ambassadors," a name given to Jewish guest speakers from New York.

I was afraid that I would be in the hands of a nudnik, but he appeared to be a most charming and exciting companion. Riding in his car through the town I learned that he had come to this part of the land three generations ago; he knew fantastic stories of the times when Jewish migrants of fifty and sixty years ago who had left their shtetlech in Eastern Europe, went through the hell of the "Island of Tears" and of "Castle Garden" in New York, from where they were sent here by Jewish emigration organizations. Many ran away from this wilderness to larger Jewish communities but some became intoxicated by the smell of oil and remained. The people I was to speak to were mostly the children of these first adventurers.

After a sumptuous supper the old gentleman, who looked as if he came out of the Forsythe saga, brought me to the home of the president of the local "branch." Five men, the whole executive board, were waiting for me. They were all elderly men and they all smoked long and thick cigars. They offered me one and I accepted. And so, sitting around the table, with the cigars in our mouths, I found out that there was a change in the schedule. The lecture which was supposed to be held on Sunday, was postponed until Monday. This interfered with my timetable—for I was on a tour in the South—and I asked for the reason.

"We can't have the lecture on Sunday," explained the president, "because we'll most probably have a funeral that day."

This "most probably" sounded very unusual.

"How's that?" I asked, "What does this 'most probably' mean?"

—It means, said the president, that our treasurer, Genosse Cymerman, had a heart seizure and we don't expect much 'naches' from him.

—Much—what?

—Naches, said the president. Don't you know what 'naches' means?

—I don't see the connection, I said.

—The connection is this, explained the president. Today is Wednesday. Genosse Cymerman may hold on till Thursday. Or let's say—till Friday. Since there are no funerals on Saturday, he'll be buried on Sunday. Ergo: the lecture must be put off till Monday.

—Gentlemen, I said, aren't you taking a too fatalistic view? How can one talk like this about a man who's still alive? The president took his cigar out of his mouth and chuckled:

—Our enemies should be so alive as Cymerman is. He's 87. This is his sixth heart attack. What else do you want?

I had nothing more to say and the lecture was put off till Monday. But the president's precaution was fortunately exaggerated. Before I left the town I visited Genosse Cymerman in the hospital. He felt fine. Someone must have told him why the lecture had been postponed for he said, squinting an eye: "When you come here next time, I'll be your chairman. And if we postpone the date again it won't be because of me, but because of that son-of-a-bitch, the president."

Another time a somewhat similar event had a more cheerless ending. It was the only time in my career that I refused to give a talk. It was in a small town in New Jersey. When I came to the address, the organization occupied an entire one-story building in the middle of a garden. I saw that the door was locked, all the window blinds were drawn, there wasn't a living soul on the whole block.

I checked the advertisement in the newspaper and on the invitation again. There was no mistake—the date was right and the address was right. Such a thing had never happened before; even if the public had chosen not to come, someone of the committee must have been there, at least the secretary. I walked around the house several times, then sat on the verandah of the wooden house and began to think about going back to New York.

Suddenly two huge, private buses drove up and halted before the building. The doors opened and a crowd of men and women began coming out and rushing toward the door. A small swarthy man ran ahead of everybody and unlocked the door. I was watching the scene in amazement. What happened? Was it the custom of this "branch" to collect the audience from their homes and bring them all by bus? I followed the crowd and entered the house. I searched for the little man with the keys and walked up to him.

—You must be the secretary, I said.

—I am.

—I'm the lecturer.

—So I gathered.

He opened the door to a little office where I stepped in. He came in behind me followed by the chairman and his deputy. The chairman seemed to be impatient and said: "Let's go. The people are already in the hall."

I was ready to go, but I couldn't conceal my delight: "You have a beautiful custom," I said, "to bring the public by bus."

The secretary looked at the chairman and remained silent. The deputy said: "This isn't a custom. We're all coming from a funeral."

I must have made a terrible face for he explained gently: "One of our distinguished members died. The whole branch went to the funeral."

I shivered:—You mean to say . . .

—That we're all coming back from the cemetery.

I shuddered again:—And you want me to talk now to the people about "The Hilarity of Jewish Humor?"

The chairman said thoughtfully:—Couldn't you make it a little less funny?

I got up:—Sorry, gentlemen. You must put it off to a later date.

"Don't be silly," said the secretary. "You'll never have such a big audience as you have today. We haven't had such a crowd in years."

But the other two agreed that I should perhaps go home and I left carrying the briefcase with the thesis of the lecture.

THIRTY YEARS AFTER

I find traveling by train more relaxing than boarding airport buses and waiting for planes. So I preferred to take a train to this midwest city although it took a full night to travel. The leaders of the Jewish organization who invited me to lecture were elegant enough to reserve a room for me in a posh downtown hotel and sufficiently discreet to leave me alone a whole day. I had enough time to rest, take a stroll around the city, visit the local museum, have lunch in a Chinese restaurant, and then return to the hotel for another rest before my lecture.

About four o'clock the telephone in the room rang.

—Are you Mr. Shulman?—The voice was that of a woman.

—Yes.

—I read in the English-Jewish weekly about your coming. Would you mind if I asked you something?

I was used to all sorts of nudniks and said: "Not at all."

—Did you ever live in Warsaw?

She spoke with a ringing Polish accent: rolling "r's," hard "l's" and long "a's."

—Yes—I said—I lived in Warsaw.

—Forgive me. I'm probably wrong. Were you, in the last two years before the war, a student in the School of Journalism?

—Yes.

—I saw that you're using the name Abraham. Didn't you at that time call yourself Abrasha?

—Yes. How do you know? Who are you?

—There was a girl in your class. It's too long for you, of course, to remember. Her name was Tosia.

My hand began to tremble. So did my voice:

—I do remember. What happened to her?

—She's alive.

—Where is she?

—In this city.

—Impossible.

Trembling must be contagious, for her voice too began to quiver:

—It's possible. It's me. I am Tosia.

—You?

There came a short but long-lasting silence. She was the first to break it:

—It's over thirty years . . .

—My God.

—Would you like to see me?

—Yes. Of course. We must.

—Remember—she said—it's thirty years.

—So?

—You'll have to be tolerant.

—Tolerant?

—I'm scared to show myself.

—How did you survive?

—The natural way. By miracles.

—Why did you bury yourself in this faraway town?

—Far from where?

—Are you—married?

—I'll tell you when I see you.

—When?

—I live an hour's drive from your hotel. Wait in the lobby.

I put down the receiver and remained motionless. Tosia!

The thirty years began to shrink until they vanished. The room filled with the past emerging from everywhere, mostly from the dark corners. Tosia! The girl with the green eyes framed in black eyelashes. Tosia the "goddess." That was what we called her and the way we loved her—with veneration and homage. She was a poet and because of her we all became poets. Had she been a ropewalker we would have become ropewalkers. Or jugglers. Or chimney sweeps. She, of course, was writing poetry on many subjects, while the theme of our verses was one only.

The strangest thing of all was that while we were in love with her, each of us was also in love with his own girl. For she, being as unattainable as an idol, was to be worshipped; any thought of possessing her would be blasphemy. She was thoroughly beautiful—nature seldom ventures into such an extravaganza of magnanimity. She was young—we were all, of course, young, but not like her—she was the essence of youth. She lived with her parents in an independent part of a luxurious apartment where she was holding, as we called it humorously "salons." A la Madame Récamier. But while the French lady, after the exuberance of food and brilliance of talk, picked her favorite man to accompany her to the bedroom, nothing of that sort was to happen here.

Only once did I come to her by myself and then not intentionally. She was alone. After I came in she did a thing she'd never done before. She locked the door and extinguished all the lights except one. She invited me to sit on the same couch as she. Was I comfortable? Would I care for a glass of wine? I was comfortable and we had a drink. Would I like to see an album of her photos as a child? I expressed a tremendous interest in every photo and snapshot. I studied each in the trembling lamplight. I looked at the details, commented on the qualities, admired

59

the texture, praised the lights and shadows. I compared some of them to Rembrandt, found in others a resemblance to Franz Hals, related others to the Polish painter Mateyko. The album contained many dozens of pictures and I was heroically prepared to go over the whole lot with patience and care. She was sitting close to me, helping me hold the photos against the light; this compelled her to come still closer, to touch my hand, to lean over me in a way that I could feel the warmth of her body, but I had sufficient strength to ignore it. Finally, holding before my eyes a photo of herself as a tot, completely undressed she asked: "Wasn't I cute?" I answered moronically: "It's a perfect Renoir." It was then that she moved away, got up, put on all the lights and asked if it wasn't time for me to go home, for it was the habit of the janitors in Warsaw to shut the gates at 11 o'clock.

All this happened thirty years ago and now, after all this time, I was going to see her. I showered, shaved, and combed what remained of my hair, still parting it on the left. I put on a white shirt with a black suit but changed my mind and changed into a pair of light slacks and a sport jacket. It was exactly an hour after she called. I left the room and rode down the elevator to the lobby.

It was crammed with people. There were a few convention meetings, and dozens of men, all dressed alike, were milling around with conspicuous cards pinned to their lapels announcing their names and titles. My heart pounded as I began scanning the faces of the women. Which one was she? I picked a strategic position, under a pillar, from which I could observe without being seen. I slowly went over the women's faces, eliminating—how tragically cruel—the faces of the younger women. I eliminated all the ones of 18, 20, 25, 30 and even 40. I made a quick mathematical addition: in 1938 she was twenty; now, thirty years later, she couldn't be under the full fifty.

This was a horrible piece of arithmetic, but such is the rule of addition, which has no room for exceptions.

I again went over the faces of the ladies resting a while longer on those that would be classified as middle-aged and even elderly. In what degree had the years destroyed the "extravaganza of magnanimity?" I looked at one of the plush covered armchairs and suddenly saw her. My God!

She was sitting wrapped in a mink coat with a small round hat of plastic flowers on her undulated hair. She was still thin and slim and her face still held on to the remnants of the past; but they were remnants, what a ghastly word! She was sitting with her profile to me. I could see one eye only—it was still green and framed in black, but the green was pale and the black was faded. I was now supposed to take a few steps forward, tap her cheerfully on her shoulder and exclaim with joy "Tosia!" and add the most horrendous lie: "You look wonderful. You've hardly changed." I was ready to take the most difficult step of my life. I had another look at her. She was sitting motionless, waiting with a frozen heart for this cruel encounter. I gave her a last look, whispering to myself, in French "Mon Dieu," and then in Yiddish "Reboyne shel oylom." I gathered every ounce of courage and stepped to her, but it was at this very second that I really saw her.

No, it wasn't this disintegrated scarecrow sitting on the armchair. The real Tosia was standing across the hall, in a shadowed niche, between two Pepsi machines. She wasn't exactly as she'd been in the past, but she was almost the same. Still youthful, still slim, still beautiful with a new radiance that evolved naturally from the old. The spider of time who does his wrinkling job of destruction was in her case generous. She didn't look thirty years older, she looked thirty years wiser. And the wisdom was resting on still delicate and still charming features.

A heavy stone, as a Yiddish saying goes, fell from my chest. I started towards her, this time ready to say the same prepared text, but with total honesty. We were separated by no more than a single step when I saw something that made me shudder.

She was standing there, her eyes fixed upon something with open horror. What was she seeing? I followed her eyes and saw the object of her abhorrence. She was looking at a small withered man with a ravished face—his eyes were dead, his mouth a decayed cavity, the skin over his face a sickly yellow. And he was bald! And he had grotesquely protruding ears, large and pointed like the ears of a donkey. She looked at him with quavering lips but nevertheless determined to go over, tap him on his hunched shoulder and gaily exclaim: "Abrasha!" and follow it with a monstrous perversion of truth.

I nimbly took a step forward and caught her before she made her desperate plunge.

A PUZZLING APPLAUSE

The subject of my talk was the "Three Classics of Yiddish Literature: Mendele Moicher Seforim, I. L. Peretz and Sholom Aleichem." The audience was receptive and there was a general atmosphere of attentiveness. But when, after describing the life and works of Mendele Moicher Seforim, I concluded with the sentence: "Mendele Moicher Seforim died in 1917," the audience broke out into loud applause. I stared in astonishment. Why the applause? The fact that he died in 1917? But I had no time for speculation and continued with the second of the Big Three, I. L. Peretz. Again the audience listened attentively, and as I finished this part with the information that Peretz died in 1915, there was again, spontaneous applause, louder even than for Mendele. Once again I was bewildered.

I now proceeded to give a humorous account of the works of Sholom Aleichem and drew many chuckles and laughs. But as soon as I said that he died in New York in 1916, the applause again erupted.

Pious Jews leave unanswerable questions till the time of the Messiah. They say: "The Messiah will resolve such problems and queries." I must add my own puzzlement over this applause for the coming of the Messiah.

A LECTURE—
A CALAMITY

The lecture was a calamity from the very beginning. I arrived by train to this remote town and nobody was waiting at the station as previously arranged. This was in itself aggravating. I called the secretary and his tone was cool and unfriendly. He advised me to get a cab and go to a hotel where the executive committee had reserved a room. He said he would come and pick me up shortly before the lecture.

The hotel was a dilapidated affair. The bellboy was an elderly half-blind and completely deaf gentleman who took me to my sixth-floor room in an antiquated elevator operated by a rope. The room was small. The walls were covered with black wallpaper, and the floor was waxed with some black shiny wax. There were only three pieces of furniture: a black wardrobe, a black rocking chair and a huge bed covered with a black spread.

My mood was already gloomy, and was further depressed by the arrival of the secretary, a silent and irritable man, who didn't even try to suppress his impatience. He took me in his car—a black limousine—to the hall which was half filled with a few dozen elderly people. The chairman introduced me briefly and then sat back, already bored. The subject of my lecture, "The Magic of Jewish Folklore," required a different setting. I must have looked miserable, because the majority of the listeners sat fidgeting in their seats. Before the lecture, which dragged hopelessly, was over, a part of the audience began to sneak out through a back door. One of them was the secretary. After I finished, the chairman waited until everybody had gone. He then put out the lights, led me out through the front door into a completely deserted street, advised me to get a cab and disappeared.

I returned to the hotel room in a black mood, lay down in the black bed (what gave my wife the idea of putting a black pair of pajamas into the suitcase?) and as soon as I closed my eyes, I sank into a series of black nightmares.

It must have been no more than six in the morning when my telephone rang. I grabbed the black receiver. "Genosse Shulman?" "Yes." "This is the chairman." "Yes?" "The chairman of your last night's lecture." "What happened?" "Nothing special. I just wanted to tell you that your lecture was a catastrophe."

"And to tell me this you wake me at six in the morning? You couldn't wait till later?" "I could," he said, "but I wanted to be the first."

AN INSPIRED LECTURE

I entered the Hall and was pleasantly surprised. A huge audience filled every seat around linen covered tables. The majority consisted of young people and included even a number of teenagers. But I also noticed in a corner a small orchestra consisting of four instruments: a guitar, a cello, a saxophone and a cluster of drums. It became evident that the main "cultural program" was a dance and that my lecture was a mere appendix demanded by the Central Office to demonstrate an interest in Yiddish culture.

I reached the platform at the moment when the chairman was having a lively argument with a representative of the younger people. Should the program start with the dance, the lecture being squeezed into one of the musical intervals, or should it begin with the lecture and the dance follow without interruption? I noticed with satisfaction that neither had suggested a third alternative—that I should deliver my lecture while the people were dancing. The young man was an aggressive type, but despite the fact that the chairman was in every respect his opposite, the chairman won. It was agreed that the evening would start with the lecture, "A Century of Modern Yiddish Literature."

The chairman beamed with triumph but his victory was mixed with apprehension. While he was leading me toward the lectern, he asked in a whisper: "By the way, what is the subject?"

"A Century of Modern Yiddish Literature."

"Do me a favor," he said, "limit yourself to fifty years. I'll find you another opportunity to talk about the other fifty."

He then began his introduction.

"My friends, we are beginning the evening with a very interesting lecture by our guest speaker. If there is anybody in this hall who doesn't feel like staying, he should leave at once and go to the adjoining room which is provided with a buffet of sandwiches and soft drinks."

No sooner had he said these words than all the younger people jumped from their seats and ran toward an open door as though a fire alarm had been sounded. The teenagers ran the fastest, but they were immediately followed by older ones. Some women ran holding children by their hands. I stood behind the lectern and watched the exodus. After a few minutes the hall looked as if it had been hit by a tornado. All that remained of the big crowd were a few elderly couples, the representative of the younger generation whose reason for staying soon became obvious, and the four musicians who remained for the practical purpose of tuning their instruments.

This created some strange effects. The saxophones suddenly began a nostalgic wail while I mentioned the name of the poet Itzik Manger, and a string broke on the guitar at the moment when I mentioned the "literature of the Holocaust destruction."

As soon as I finished, the young man ran toward the door and cried out: "It's over. You can all come back!"

The hall was filled in a minute. And when the chairman took the microphone to "thank the speaker for his most inspired lecture," I received from the public one of the most gratifying rounds of applause in my entire career.

QUESTION TIME

At an early stage I learned that Yiddish audiences come not only to listen. To some listeners the lecture is an opportunity for showing off their own erudition. These are the lecture crashers who attempt to transform the lecture into their own show, not in the form of heckling, which would be unforgiveable during the ritual of a "cultural event." The "crashers" sit patiently throughout the lecture. Their time arrives when the chairman announces that "now the speaker will reply to questions." This gives them the cue to leap on the prey. Often the chairman, who is aware of this possibility, makes it clear that "a question should be a question." This may sound tautological, but it is really necessary. "No comments, no speeches, nothing but a brief question." This is a strict warning to any potential nudnik, who may seize the opportunity to deliver his own speech. The chairman's warning is intended to protect the audience. It is not his business to protect the speaker against individuals who sit quietly with javelins in their sleeves, ready to throw them at the speaker's head as soon as the question period is announced. Are they vicious? God forbid. Their only aim is to lacerate the speaker. Their intention is to light the spark of their own brilliance, in a brief moment of glory.

"The speaker was quite right in saying that the writer Zalmen Schneyur was a genius, but has he forgotten that

Gogol, too, was a writer of great talent?" The shrewdness of such a question is threefold. "Quite right" patronizes. "Has he forgotten" is a way of saying "of course he hasn't forgotten, he is simply an ignoramus." And the introduction of the unrelated name of Gogol is to demonstrate the questioner's own scholarship. More dangerous are the ones who come with the open intention of rending the speaker to pieces. These people come with questions prepared in advance which can be pinned to anything. For instance: if the lecture was about the "Christological elements in the writings of Sholom Asch," the question may be, "What, according to the speaker, would Kropotkin say of Asch's Nazarene?" The first time I was asked such a question, I called for a repetition. This in itself was a mistake. It intimated that I was not at all or only vaguely aware of Piotre Alexandrovitch Kropotkin, who for over half a century was the leader of the Russian and international anarchists. But still worse than hesitation is the blank and sincere answer: "I don't know." This is the unforgiveable blunder. The Cultural Center in New York has no right to send speakers whose minds contain less than the latest edition of the Encyclopaedia Britannica. Nobody is willing to pay an admission fee for "I don't know." A question unanswered is a blemish not only on the lecturer, but also throws a shadow of doubt on the integrity of the whole organization. The fact is that even the Encyclopaedia Britannica does not suffice to provide answers to some of the queries. Was Columbus a Jew? Was Tolstoy acquainted with the Kabalah? Why didn't Heinrich Heine visit Eretz Israel? Was Dostoyevski sincere when he wrote the Brothers Karamazov? Of what disease did Spinoza die? Is it true that Napoleon was circumcised?

Often the person who asks a question is not in the least interested in the answer. It may even happen that after winning the respect of the audience with the quality of his

JUDAISM AND SOCIALISM

The invitation came from a group of Jewish socialists in a small community in Connecticut who were known to me from a journal they stubbornly published in New York. The socialism they preached was of an ancient and romantic sort. The theme of my lecture was "The forgotten Jewish tribes," a report of my encounters with Jewish communities in exotic places like Iran, Morocco, Afghanistan, Tunisia and Yemen. The lecture was of a descriptive character, sprinkled with anecdotes, but the idea behind it was the eternal problem of the "Jewish Mystique."

I finished my lecture somewhat exhausted but satisfied. I had managed to hold the attention of the elderly but alert audience for over an hour. As soon as I finished, the chairman got up and announced the "question period." I sat back ready to answer any and all questions. However, the very first question had nothing to do with the subject. It was designed to put the speaker in his place.

A tall man with a head of silvery hair, dressed in a sport jacket, a checkered shirt and a strawberry colored bow tie, got up and asked in a challenging voice:

"Mr. Speaker, what comes first, Judaism or socialism?"

His question was terse. It was also loaded with pitfalls.

71

From the silence that followed I sensed that whatever my answer, part of the audience would be antagonized. Judaism comes first? What about socialism? Socialism comes first? What about Yiddishkeit? There was no way of getting out of it by saying: "It's up to your own judgment." The problem was of basic importance and it was expected that a lecturer sent by the Central Department of Culture in New York should not stumble over such a question. The man who posed the question now sat with an expression of triumph; obviously I wasn't his first victim. I could also see from the looks of the audience that this was not a simple matter of answering a question, but rather a test of the speaker's intelligence, wit, acumen, perspicacity and his Jewish and social awareness.

The room, which until that moment had been a pleasant arena for my eloquence, had changed into a pit in which I had been entrapped and thrown to the lions. When I looked down at the floor I could literally see a heap of skulls and bones of previous speakers who had been invited to speak by this group, and were exposed to that impossible question.

But was it impossible? Fortunately, at the instant when I saw the open mouth of the abyss, I also heard the flapping of wings. They came from my personal angel. And the angel whispered into my ear the only sensible answer. The man in the checkered shirt looked challengingly at me ready to plunge in the dagger, but I now looked back with defiance. I answered his question in the customary Jewish manner: with another question. "Do you consider yourself a Jew?"

—Of course!

—You also consider yourself a socialist?

—Naturally.

—How old were you when you became a socialist?

—Twelve.—His answer sounded like a verse from the International.
—And how old were you when you became a Jew?
He looked at me with suspicion.
—What do you mean?
The audience held their breath. It was evident that they were all on his side.
—How old were you when they performed on you the act which is called the Covenant of Abraham with God?
—You mean circumcision?
—Yes, I mean circumcision.
—When I was eight days old.
—There you are—I said. You can see for yourself which comes first.
The man with the silvery hair looked confused for a while, but the majority of the audience applauded and he eventually joined them.

A MAN WITH A STEEL HOOK

It was a ten story building close to the Public Library in Manhattan. My lecture ("Social Elements in Jewish Humor") was to be held in one of the rooms on the top floor. The whole building consisted of such rooms rented out to Jewish "Landsmanshaften," fraternal orders and cultural groups. It also contained larger halls for anniversaries, weddings and Bar Mitzvahs.

The lobby behind the front door was brightly lit and empty. I walked straight to the elevator and pressed the button. At the very last moment, when I was already in the elevator and had already reached for the button number Ten, another man jumped inside, the doors closed, and the elevator began its slow and torturous ride upward.

My companion was a huge man, a colossus, no less than seven feet tall, with enormously wide shoulders. I would gladly skip the color of his skin, but it was his color as much as anything else which created for me the suspense of the next few minutes. My first instinct, in this city of muggings, was to leave the elevator, pretending that I had just come down. But the elevator doors shut like the lid of a coffin before I could implement such a strategy. We were standing close to each other—there being no room for comfortable distances—but the beating of my heart was still regular, my breathing was calm. My panic had not as yet increased the flow of adrenaline.

I was calm, collected, waiting. Would it be the blade of a knife or the barrel of a gun? Would he say simply: "Quick, your wallet!" Or would he utter a more flamboyant command containing words which I could not repeat later in a middle-class company?

I was quite prepared to hand my wallet over and add as a premium a small gilded watch, a pair of gold cuff links and a tiny lighter—which I bought for a friend at Paris' Orly airport and later decided to keep for myself. I was also ready to throw in a Parker pen of the latest style, which I had seen advertised in "Esquire" magazine. But I knew too well that neither the precious things themselves nor the dignified manner of surrendering them would save me from a clout on the head.

Muggers have their own etiquette. Hitting the victim on the head is the most practical way of saving a mugger from unnecessary trouble. It prevents the victim from crying out; it makes it impossible for him, after the fact, to chase the assailant, shouting: "Help!" or "Police!" or "Stop that man!" It also induces a temporary blackout which in potential confrontation may make the victim unable to recognize his assailant.

The elevator reached the first floor and I was waiting for one of three possibilities: a clout on the head, the glitter of a knife blade, or the cold touch of a gun—all this accompanied by an X-rated whisper. When none of the three happened, I ventured a sideways glance and I couldn't help but smile at my naiveté. The man was not only a giant, but he had also only one good arm. The other was an artificial limb, the greater part of which was hidden inside his sleeve, while the rest hung below his cuff in the form of an enormous steel hook.

Keeping my eyes lowered, I could see this hook in all its dimensions. It had the shape and size of the meat hooks from which slaughterers hang the carcasses of cattle. It was now clear why the man didn't use a knife or gun. Being endowed with such a hook, the use of any other weapon was simply ludicrous. The idea that he would suddenly raise his steel hook and let it down by the force of gravity was almost hilarious in its simplicity.

In the meantime, the elevator had passed the second and third floors and was heading with the speed of a drugged snail toward the fourth. What was keeping him? What the hell was he waiting for? Was he, in addition to being a hold-upnik, also a sadist? Or was he a connoisseur of the moribund?

Four, five, six. I was suddenly struck—not with the hook—with an idea. Should I, perhaps, instead of passively standing and waiting, take the initiative. In other words: should I get my wallet out of my back pocket and hand it over to him with an elegant bow? "Here is my wallet, sir." And immediately afterwards present him with the watch. "Genuine Swiss. Omega. Waterproof, self-winding."

The elevator crawled toward the seventh floor. Then the eighth. The man's intentions were becoming as clear as daylight. His plan was to get me to the top floor, perform the ritual with the hook, drag my corpse onto the landing, where there was small possibility of its being found, and unperturbed, ride the elevator back to the lobby, get to the street and disappear in the crowd.

Tenth floor. The elevator stopped. The door opened. The giant stepped aside and let me out first. Very logical. He was trotting behind me. Also logical. The passage was long and empty. The scene was set and all the props were in place: the victim, the executioner, the weapon. I kept on marching, remembering Rubashov from Koestler's "Darkness at Noon." Would the hook fall in front of the door marked with the red lamp "Exit"? Naturally. It would be easier to drag a body onto the landing. About half a yard from the exit door, I recalled the first sentence of the Hebrew prayer of those about to die. I am not a believer, but none of my friends, who trust my agnosticism, was there to watch; so I could freely, and with no fear of being accused of hypocrisy, intone: "Oshamnu, Bogadnu, Gozalnu."

I arrived at the exit. Boom! Boom? No. Not yet. Sadism with a touch of humor? I passed the exit and was approaching the door of the room where I was supposed to hold the lecture. Aha! Now the strategy of the fellow was becoming obvious. What he planned was not an individual slaying, not the robbing of a single victim, but a collective holdup. I saw it clearly. As soon as I'll open the door, the giant would force himself into the room, finish off the whole gathering with a few strokes of the hook, and after heaping the corpses behind the speaker's platform, he would help himself to the valuables from their pockets and leave. To my horror, the door of the lecture room stood open and the chairman was waiting on the threshold with a wide smile on his lips. But, curiously, the smile wasn't for me. He was smiling to somebody over my head. To whom? To the hold-upnik? To the giant with the lethal hook?

"Do you know each other?" the chairman asked.

"I haven't the pleasure," the colossus said and looked down at me. He extended his left, natural hand and told me his name. To anyone interested, Zachariah Lincoln was the chairman of the local chapter or the Urban League. He had been invited to address the members of the branch on the subject of brotherhood.

After he spoke, he remained to listen to my lecture, "Social elements in Jewish Humor." It had neither the elements nor the humor.

A MACABRE RIDE

The train pulled up at the station and I picked up my briefcase with the thesis of the lecture about Shalom Aleichem. I walked in the midst of a big crowd along the platform looking for a friend who was an executive member of the organization that had arranged the talk. But instead, a stranger stopped me as I emerged into the hall of the station: "You must be Genosse Shulman?"

He was middle-aged, had a black coat, a black derby-hat, and black gloves. And a black mustache. "Black" in Yiddish is "Schwartz." His name was neither Schwartz-man nor Schwartzer, yet it belonged to a close semantic family: Dunkelman, the Man of Darkness.

We walked to the parking lot where he had left his car. He told me that he's a devoted reader of everything that's humorous, and that Shalom Aleichem was his idol. He believed with Shalom Aleichem, he said, that "laughter is healthy." But he added something puzzling. "For others humor is a matter of taste, for me it's a vital necessity."

"Vital?"—I asked.

"Vital," he repeated, "considering my profession."

He didn't volunteer anything more and I didn't think it proper to press him. It was a mild, wintery day; white snow covered the ground. He marched ahead of me and he looked like a big black bird. Or rather like the black clothed executioner of the French Revolution who was reverently called "Monsieur." I have little inclination to mysticism but this man in the black attire—did I mention that he was also holding a black umbrella?—evoked in me dark thoughts. The softness of the snow added to the atmosphere of mystery—his soundless footsteps made him almost unreal. He seemed like a character who had walked out of an Ingmar Bergman movie.

We came to his car. He turned to me and smiled. This would have dispelled my apprehension, except for something terrible: the limousine before which he stopped was long, black, and had silky grey curtains in the back windows. Without saying a word, Mr. Dunkelman motioned me to enter. As I stepped in I could see the interior behind the front seats: an empty, rectangular space surrounded by three rows of upholstered seats. My reflex was to withdraw and run, but Mr. Dunkelman had already started the motor and we began to move.

Mr. Dunkelman was driving and I held my hand across my mouth so he couldn't hear my teeth chattering. Up to this moment I had thought that the expression "hair standing on end" was a poetical metaphor; now I knew better. I remembered what Mr. Dunkelman had said about the vital need for laughter in his profession. I shut both eyes not to get a glimpse of what might be going on behind my back. But I could feel cold skeleton fingers emerging from the back and approaching my throat.

I was also afraid to look at the man at the wheel. Was Mr. Dunkelman really Mr. Dunkelman? And was he really taking me to a place where I was going to lecture? The street along which we were now riding ended in a copse of trees, beyond which, I was certain, was a Jewish cemetery; a minute from now, Mr. Dunkelman would drive his limousine through a gate to an open hole in the ground surrounded by the public which was supposed to come to my lecture and which, instead, came to bury the speaker.

Mr. Dunkelman who had been so talkative at the railway station was now sitting completely silent. The snow made the wheels move in stillness. All I could hear was a rattling. I couldn't make out whether this was my teeth or the skeleton bones from the interior of the hearse.

I thought of the custom of pious Jews to wear a Talise Katan, or fringes with which they can chase away unholy spirits. I was ready at this moment to offer half my possessions for such fringes. I looked out through the side windows to have a glimpse of the passerby: were they surprised to see a funeral riding at this late hour? Were they taking off their hats or were they crossing themselves?

In vain did I search my memory for the prayer of the dying. All I remembered was the blessing Jews say when they drink wine: Boyre pri hagofen. This had no connection with my present ordeal. But I said it nevertheless; it was better than nothing.

The limousine suddenly made an abrupt turn, we found ourselves on a brightly lit Avenue and stopped before a building carrying the sign: Jewish Community Center. My friend who had been supposed to meet me at the station was waiting here. He greeted me happily and explained that he hadn't come to the station because Mr. Dunkelman who was a great fan of my humorous stories in the "Jewish Daily Forward," wanted to have the mitzvah. I asked faintly: "Who is Mr. Dunkelman?" He was, as I had guessed the ower of the biggest funeral parlor in town. He had the best clientele. He also had a keen sense of humor.

Which was true. For when I looked at the audience from the height of the podium, Mr. Dunkelman was sitting in the front row, vis à vis the mike, I tried to avoid looking in his direction, but I couldn't help hearing him laugh. He was laughing like a horse. A black-clothed horse, pulling and old-fashioned hearse with lanterns.

A BANQUET

Subways on a Sunday afternoon are practically empty. Few people travel at this hour from Brooklyn to Manhattan. It was comfortable and quiet—an ideal atmosphere to sit back and go over the highlights of my speech.

At one of the stations a passenger entered and I recognized the well-known Yiddish critic, whom I shall call Birenboym. He was wearing his oversized fur coat which made him look like a bear walking on his hind legs. He was going to the same place that I was, to a midtown hotel where a Yiddish club had organized a banquet for a Jewish poet, Katz (the name is fictional), on the occasion of his 60th birthday. Birenboym and I were the two speakers. As soon as I saw him I cried out: "Birenboym!" and invited him to sit next to me.

He walked over in silence. His face was sullen, he looked gloomy and downcast.

—What's the matter, Birenboym? You look as if your ship of sour milk has gone under.

My Yiddish idiom didn't change his gloom.

—It's terrible—he grunted—It's a lousy business.

—You mean the weather?

—I mean the boring thing they've dragged me into.

I pretended not to understand:

—You mean the banquet?

—You may call it a banquet. To me it's worse than a funeral.

—Why a funeral? What's wrong with celebrating a poet who has turned sixty?

—There's nothing wrong with a poet who has turned anything. As long as he's a poet.

—You mean that Katz isn't?

Birenboym gave me a poisonous look:

—If he is a poet, then I'm a belly dancer. He is the greatest cripple that our literature has ever produced. He is the most incompetent, the most emasculated poetical invalid I have known in my whole lifetime.

—But some of our critics put him in the front row of our poetry.

—Some of our critics should be put in the same row and summarily shot.

—But surely, Birenboym, you cannot deny that he has an unusual language.

—Unusual is the right word—hissed Birenboym. The originality of his language consists in the fact that he has no idea of syntax or grammar. Any imbecile can take a normal sentence, scratch out every third word, distort the rest and get an original style.

—But the metaphors!

—He has two sorts of metaphors—barked Birenboym— Fifty percent are stolen from Chaim Nachman Bialik and the other fifty are pinched from Moyshe Leyb Halperin.

—And yet—I said feebly—Hasn't he introduced some unconventional themes?

—That's true—grinned Birenboym—He's as unconventional as garbage in rossel-soup.

I began to feel more resentful:

—If that's what you think of him, then why go to the banquet at all?

—I'm being dragged by the head. I'm being pulled by the ears. He called me a hundred times. His wife called me two hundred. He told all his friends and relatives to keep calling me. I'm being lynched. I'm terroized. I'm raped. He looked straight into my eyes:

—And what about you? Are you telling me that you're going of your own will?

Fortunately the subway arrived and we got off.

The hall was crowded and brightly lit. The poet, dressed in "black tie" was sitting in his honorable place beaming with happiness. The chairman made a brief introduction. Birenboym was to speak first. He sat at the other end of the table his head lowered, his face dark like a lantern in a shroud of crepe.

The chairman called his name. He walked heavily over to the mike. My heart shrunk. I saw him stop. He pulled out a few white sheets from his pocket and began to read.

I can't recall everything he said, but to the best of my recollection he said, more or less, this: "Katz is by his poetical blood related to Homer, to Baudelaire and to Alexander Pushkin. . . . The Greeks are proud of their Acropolis, the Romans of their Forum Romanum, the French of their cathedrals, we are proud of Katz. . . . The highest peak in the Himalayas is Mount Everest, the highest in the Alps is Mont Blanc, the highest in Turkestan is Tangri Khan, our apex is Katz. . . . Katz is our crown, our symbolic fringes, he is the Mezuzah on the gates of our poetical kingdom. . . . "

After his speech came an interval. My own speech opened the second half. When the whole thing was finished I intended to travel home together with Birenboym, but I couldn't find him. As soon as I entered the subway car I saw him in his oversized fur sitting in a corner with a sunken head.

—What's the matter?—I asked—Why this gloom?

83

—Why not?—he grunted—to lose a whole Sunday afternoon for such a literary cripple.

—But, Birenboym! Didn't you say yourself . . .

—Say-shmay—he shrugged his shoulders, closed his eyes and looked like a ship with black masts.

YIDDISH IN A REFORMED TEMPLE

Most lectures are arranged through the Central Office. But this one came directly from the "consumer." A lady called me up and presented herself as the secretary of a temple in Long Island. Would I be willing to give a talk?

This was the first time I had been approached by a temple and I asked for more details. Did they expect a talk on a religious subject? "Oh no," said the woman. The congregation consisted of people who are second or third generation Americans, not one of them speaks Yiddish, but each has a vague knowledge. They heard it from their grandparents, fewer from their parents, and some from Leon Rosten's "The Joy of Yiddish." "However," the secretary said, "this isn't the main thing." I asked what was the main thing and she explained:

—There's a suddenly arisen desire of the majority of the congregation members, particularly of the young, to learn the language. Why? It could be a wish for identity. A desire to know one's origins. An awakening of a nonverbalized yearning after seeing "The Fiddler on the Roof," or after reading a story by Isaac Bashevis Singer.

I asked: Suppose I accept and give this talk in Yiddish. Will they understand? Or will I talk to the walls?

—Whatever the case, the lady said, please accept. It's a mitzvah.

A mitzvah is a thing against which there can be no arguments. We fixed the date and on the appointed Sunday, I took all the trains and buses necessary and arrived at the temple building. In front of the building were two tablets of stone with engraved Roman letters standing for the Ten Commandments. I hesitated before one of three doors and opened what seemed at the first moment to be the wrong one, for inside were people who couldn't, because of their age, be a gathering for a lecture in Yiddish.

My reflex was to withdraw, but my entrance was noticed by a young woman. "You must be the speaker," she said, "I'm the secretary who spoke to you on the phone."

A slim man appeared at her side, the president of the temple. He was very young, too young to have achieved a position after which one can go no higher. He had a magnificent head of undulated hair, cheerful sideburns and a mustache à la Viva Villa. The secretary spoke English, but he, after greeting me with a "Baruch Habo" said, in what was intended to be Yiddish: "Ich sei eier fursitzer." I'm going to be your chairman. He said it with such pride that the three mistakes he made in four words sounded wonderfully sympathetic.

He told me that tonight's lecture was going to be an unusual event. A number of members had demanded to start a course in Yiddish and the committee had already engaged a teacher. Also, a motion had been passed to expose the members to regular Yiddish lectures. Tonight's was the first, an Act of Initiation.

He made a heroic attempt to say it all in Yiddish and I understood, if not most, at least some of it. He finished with the request that I should try to encourage the audience to participate either with questions or with comments at the conclusion of the talk. He said it all with a great deal of enthusiasm. Alas, his enthusiasm wasn't contagious. The prospect of talking to an audience to whom conservatively 70% of the content would be Chinese, was of little temptation to my ambition as a speaker. His further request to provoke a debate in a language (as I could gather from the chairman's own) that consisted of bits and pieces retained from grandparents, was even less enticing. But there was also the eagerness of the youthful chairman, my own missionary obligations as a Yiddish writer and the sight of the audience I faced a few minutes later: men and women in their twenties or thirties—alive, elegant and eager.

The chairman introduced me with a phrase that sounded like an ancient song from the Yiddish theatre: "Fraynde mayne, a sheynem guter shabes." It wasn't shabes, it was Sunday, but this detail didn't matter. What mattered was the serious, solemn and serene concentrated attention of the public.

But I was still undecided. What was the sense in speaking "al hoeytzim veal hoavonim"—to "trees and stones?" I addressed them in Yiddish "chosheve fraynt" and switched to English. I explained that although I appreciated their desire to listen to Yiddish, my own desire was that my talk should not be an exercise in linguistics but a comprehensive lecture on an important subject.

This caused an unexpected uproar. From all sides of the hall there were loud cries: "Yiddish!" The mood in the hall was such that I suggested a little test. I'd tell them a Yiddish joke and it would depend on their response whether or not I'd proceed in Yiddish.

There were a few further scattered protests but the majority considered that my suggestion was fair. I chose a joke that was a part of folklore, dealt with religion and was piquant: "The rabbi of a little shtetel looked out of his window and saw one of the Jews eating matzoh. The rabbi reprimanded him: Reb Mendel, he said, it's a sin to eat matzoh before Pesach. Eating matzoh before the seder is the same sin as making love to one's bride before the wedding.—Dear rabbi, said Reb Mendel, I tried both and they're hardly the same thing."

The test was a total triumph for the Yiddishist—the laughter was unanimous. Despite the fact that the anecdote contained four Hebrew words; "matzoh," "seder," "aveyra" and "khasene."

I was particularly pleased to see the reaction of a young blond woman who sat in the front row, vis à vis the rostrum. She was my green light and I went on with the talk. Judging from the later applause this was more than an ordinary success.

As soon as the applause subsided, a youngish man with warm and velvety black eyes, the rabbi of the temple, got up and said—in Yiddish of course—that this was a memorable evening. For "memorable" he used the word "hazkarah" which is employed at funerals: but I got the meaning. Now the chairman announced that anybody could ask questions or give their comments. There were about 200 people in the audience and such was the number of raised hands. They got up, one after the other, and began struggling with words, phrases, syntax and grammar. The spectacle was funny and moving.

It appeared from the way they pronounced the words, that their grandparents came from different parts of Poland, Lithuania, Rumania or Russia. The same word "vos" (what) was pronounced "vus," "vas," "voos" and "vues." Sitting behind the table on the podium, I could almost see the invisible threads that linked those people, born and raised on this continent, with such remote and vanished places as Vilno, Grodno, Lemberg and even

Starobyelsk and Pereyaslav. The gap was no longer there, the evening filled it.

I was especially thrilled by the young blond woman who sat in the front row and looked like a Madonna of Andrea Del Sarto. When she rose to speak I expected another pathetic striving to say a few foggily recalled words; instead, her Yiddish was fluent and had all the flavors of Galicia. She obviously saw that my reaction wasn't only amazement for her Yiddish, but also admiration for some details of her face and her lanky figure, for she added, softly and with Yiddish modesty: "I'm the rebetzin."

The rabbi appeared at her side and, with a smile in his velvety eyes, put an arm around her shoulders, meaning to demonstrate that the ancient Jewish law—in Yiddish as well as in any other language—gives to the husband exclusive rights with regard to his wife.

THE LADY
AND THE SCISSORS

This was the only time I ever came to the lecture with a cushion in my briefcase. It was small, made of taffeta and had tassels.

It happened on the last day of my tour in the South, in a city, immortalized in a Broadway musical and in many romantic songs. On the day of the lecture I had a telephone call in the hotel room from a lady who said that because of her age and state of health, she wouldn't be able to attend. She lived a few blocks away from the hotel and asked if I would kindly take a few minutes of my time and stop in at her place. She was, she said, a devoted reader of my stories in the Yiddish papers, it would give her pleasure—etc. I promised to come. I also promised to give her a book of essays of mine.

Later in the afternoon, on the way to the lecture, as I walked to her house, I passed a hardware store. A huge pair of scissors with two huge bells and sharp points caught my eye. I remembered that our old scissors at home had been lost and I went in and bought the pair. I put it in the briefcase with the lecture notes and my book of essays.

The woman lived in a two story house. Inside, the stairs were of white stone, the walls were covered with maps of

European countries. The lamps were encased in glass abat-jours painted in old-fashioned colors. On each floor, there were two massive doors with brass locks and heavy knockers. In the middle of each door, the name of the occupant was engraved on a round disk.

The woman lived on the second floor. I took hold of the knocker and rapped twice. From the other side of the door came the shuffling of feet shod in soft slippers, followed by a faint voice.

"Who is it?"

I answered, and soon I heard the turning of keys, the clicking of locks and the movement of a heavy bar. The door opened, not more than a crack, just large enough for the woman to look out. She had the head of an Australian lyrebird. She contemplated me for a while, from head to toe, stopping at my bulging briefcase. She slammed the door. Had I failed the inspection? No. Next came the rattling of a chain. The door opened wide, and the woman let me in.

The foyer was lit by small lamps with silk shades. We entered a room illuminated by lamps protruding from the walls like human arms. The floor was covered by a soft, thick rug, the walls were hung with tapestries, and the whole room was overflowing with cushions—round, square, triangular and pentagonal; leather, silk, taffeta, fur and brocade; with tassels, buttons and frills; scattered all over the floor, the chairs, the chiffonier, the mirror stand, even on the shelves among the books. Without saying a word, the woman pointed to a chair and I sank into a mountain of pillows.

I looked around. Between the tapestries on the walls hung portraits of Pushkin, Gogol, Tolstoy, Tchekhov and other pre-revolutionary Russian men of letters. The woman, fragile, thin and bony, crippled by arthritis, settled herself on another mountain of pillows. She sat close to the door, seemingly ready to jump up at any moment, flee into the hall and, if the need arose, shout in her sparrow's voice: "Police!" or "Help!" or something of that sort.

She apologized for asking me to come over. I rummaged in my mind for a joke to ease the tension, but the only thing I could think of was an ancedote about Charlotte Corday who stabbed Marat in his bathtub. I remarked that we were having a nice day and realized immediately that it was evening and that the rain was coming down in sheets. I reached for the first book on a nearby shelf, looking for an opening to conversation. It was a copy of "The Boston Strangler." From the wall, a pair of big, dark eyes looked down at me, I recognized the face of Feodor Dostoyevsky, which brought instantly to my mind the scene from "Crime and Punishment" in which the student Raskolni-koff murders old Alevna with an ax. Across the room, the woman shuddered. Could she read my mind? I sat back and tried not to move. The room was stuffy and I began to feel warm. The logical thing to do, it seemed, was to come right to the point. I seized the briefcase and whispered hoarsely: "Here's the book."

I unzipped the briefcase, it flew open and the large scissors with their threatening points fell to the floor.

Strangely, the woman didn't scream, she didn't utter a sound. She didn't leap, she didn't run into the hall shouting: "Police!" or "Help!" Neither did she fling herself through the window onto the street. Instead, she remained quite still, a good deal calmer than before. She gazed at the scissors without blinking. Her lips moved once or twice as if to say "If you have to do it, do it, but be quick about it. And please, don't soil the cushions."

I wanted to ease the atmosphere with a little laughter, but under the circumstances any laughter would have sounded like the howling of Dracula. As for picking up the scissors, that was out of the question. Suddenly I had a terrifying thought. Why not, indeed, seize hold of the shears, plunge them into her breast and put an end to it all? I recalled again the scene with Raskolnikoff and felt drops of cold sweat on my forehead.

I reached into the briefcase again to take out the book. The woman stared calmly at the briefcase, which hid my hands. I knew what she must be thinking. Not being satisifed with the scissors I was about to pull out an ax. She even smiled. The smile on her small faced seemed to say: "It's all the same to me—scissors or ax or javelin; in a moment or two I shall be hovering about in fleecy clouds, soft as my cushions, fanning the air with goose wings and strumming a harp."

Abruptly I took my hand out of the briefcase and declared in a high-pitched voice that I needed this book for the lecture. I'd mail her a copy from New York.

Bending over I picked the scissors up from the floor, rose and started to the door, I fiddled with the locks, chains, bars and bolts until the door finally opened and I threw myself into the corridor. Running down the stairs three and four at a time, I became conscious of the fact that my briefcase was bulkier than before. But I had no time for closer investigation.

Later, when I opened the briefcase at the praesidium table to start the lecture I saw the reason for its bulkiness. It was a small cushion with tassels which I had picked up together with the scissors, in my panic to depart.

ONE LECTURE AND THREE CHAIRMEN

There may be several reasons why some organizations can't afford the luxury of a lecture. One of them, the most important, is the question of attracting a public. Some organizations are simply in no position to fill their meeting hall with an audience. In these cases such a group may join hands with another. Partnerships of this kind, however temporary, have always been based on ideological kinship. There could be no union between two partners of which one would be atheist and the other religious, or one nationalist and the other cosmopolitan. No executive board would dare commit such an ideological misalliance.

However, lately these principles have become less rigid. The reason is not, God forbid, the mellowing of tenets or convictions; anarchists are still ardent anarchists, bundists are still unyielding bundists, and religious groups look at the nonreligious with the same animosity as before. Alas, the diminishing of the number of members oblige the organizations to create the most bizarre nuptial ties. In some cases they may cause quite unexpected situations.

There was no single political or cultural group in this town in Florida that could afford a "cultural event" of its own. A union was therefore formed of no less than three groups: socialists, Zionists and the congregation of an orthodox shul in which the lecture was to be held.

Since the lecture was held in a shul the socialists were obliged, against their principles, to put on paper yarmulkahs provided by the "Shames" of the shul. The congregation members were wearing their private cloth.

Because of the ephemeral character of this united front and because of the integrity of each of the participating groups, the organizers had appointed three chairmen— one to open the meeting, the other one to conduct the "question period" while the third was to summarize the "cultural event" and thank the speaker.

The lecture was scheduled to start at nine: by nine thirty only the first chairman, the socialist, had come. Since the public was getting impatient, the chairman, who considered this lack of punctuality of his two associates an affront to his political group, got up and opened the evening. His announcement was brief. He said that the subject of the talk was the poet "Itzhok Leyb Peretz" and that the speaker was "the distinguished guest from New York, Mr. Ephraim Shulman."

A member of the audience drew his attention to the fact that the speaker's name wasn't Ephraim but Abraham. The chairman apologized and said that "before giving the floor to Ephraim Shulman (the man from the audience shouted: "Abraham") I will make a few short announcements. First, that the proceeds of the bazaar of the local Kehilla were to be used to buy Israeli Bonds. An elderly man in a paper yarmulkah (a socialist) interrupted with a suggestion that the money should be given to the local Jewish hospital; another man, in a silk yarmulkah (an orthodox man) said that the money should be given to the Yeshivah.

The chairman asked them to refrain from interrupting and continued with the second announcement: the

Kehillah is organizing an excursion to Miami Beach. A man in a grey hat (a Zionist) protested that the excursion should go to Israel. A man in a paper yarmulkah jumped to his feet and cried: "Neither to Miami Beach nor Israel, but to Washington!" The chairman again asked for quiet.

Now, with the announcements disposed of, he said that he was giving the floor to "the distinguished speaker, Mr. Ephraim Shulman." Nobody corrected him and I got up to speak. At this very moment the door opened and in came a tall man in a heavy winter coat with a black fur collar. He marched directly to the table and said angrily to the first chairman: "What was the hurry? There's a fire? Why did you start without me?" He was the representative of the Zionists and was boiling like a kettle. The chairman realized that he had committed a sin which might make any future alliances impossible, so he got up and admitted that he was wrong. He apologized to the Zionist chairman (who by this time had settled himself at the center of the table) and said:

"Ladies and Gentlemen. I regret what has happened. Allow me to repeat the formalities." He said again that the subject of tonight's talk was "Itzhok Leyb Peretz" and that the speaker was "the distinguished guest from New York, Mr. Ephraim Shulman" (here a man shouted: "Abraham"). The chairman apologized and made the announcement about the bazaar, the proceeds of which would be used to buy Israeli Bonds (a member in a paper yarmulkah cried: "to the Jewish Hospital," and another one, in a cloth yarmulkah: "to the Yeshivah!"). The chairman asked them to be quiet and made the second announcement about the excursion to Miami Beach (a member of the audience, in a hat, exclaimed: "Israel!" while another one, in a paper yarmulkah shouted: "Washington!"). The chairman now gave the floor "to the distinguished speaker from New York, Mr. Ephraim Shulman" (Nobody intervened).

I collected my notes for the second time and rose to speak, when the door was flung open and in came an imposing man with a black Assyrian beard. As soon as I saw him march to the table I realized that he was the rabbi of the shul and the third chairman and I quickly put my notes back into my breast pocket. But the rabbi signaled to the chairman that there was no need to start everything from scratch. The chairman, obviously satisfied, turned to me and said: "You may proceed, Mr. Ephraim." Instead of giving the title of the lecture "Itzhok Leyb Peretz," I said "Itzhak Abraham Peretz."

MONEY MATTERS

Then there is always the delicate matter of payment. The arrangement is made in direct negotiations between the two parties without the intervention of an agent. The amount of the fee depends on a number of factors: the organization's budget, the distance from New York, etc. Most of all, it depends on the eloquence of the executive secretary and his ability to present the matter as the sacred duty of the lecturer to disseminate culture.

The presentation of the check usually takes place at the end of the evening in the presence of at least two members of the executive. It is not my nature to look inside the proffered envelope before reaching home; and there are never any surprises—either pleasant or unpleasant. Only once did it happen that I was confronted with a rather delicate situation. My lecture, for several reasons, had aroused no response from the listeners. They remained cool and no matter how hard I tried, I could establish no contact with the audience. When I finished, there was no applause, only a weak clapping from the chairman himself and an elderly lady in the front row. In short, the lecture was a flop. It was then that the executive secretary took me to a corner of the room, reluctantly pulled out his checkbook, slowly tore out a blank check and said:

"Everything considered, how much do we owe you?"

THE DANGER OF RHETORICAL QUESTIONS

I went prepared to my lecture like a French high school student to his "Bac." The subject was "H. Leywick—the great Jewish poet," and I had constructed it like a classical drama: a prologue, a plot which gradually mounted to a catastasis and then abruptly fell into an abyss from which it again rose in the fireworks of a climactical epilogue. I usually dislike theatrical effects, but Leywick, being one of my favorite poets, deserved more than just an informative account.

I also embellished the talk with oratorical ornaments. This was my first and only lecture in which I used rhetorical questions—questions that I tossed out, to catch them myself with the dexterity of a juggler. Right in the beginning, in an emotional protasis in which I described the poet's childhood, which he spent in the shadow of his terrifying copper-bearded father, I turned my profile to the audience and asked: "What was it that the child had derived from his impoverished home and his terror stricken years?" Here I allowed for a second of silence after which I turned my other profile to the public and crowned

99

the question with its answer: "A feeling for social justice and a deep-rooted complex of suffering."

I scattered the rhetorical questions throughout the lecture like glittering diamonds. But how could I suspect that this particular evening the very diamonds would become the ruin of my lecture?

The first ten minutes passed like an overture of a Mozartian opera. I started the lecture in a soft lyrical vein. "He was born into a poor little shack, and grew up surrounded by his loving caring mother and the towering figure of his Olympic father." I followed this with a description of the social background: "These were the days when new and bold ideas began knocking on the shutters of Jewish homes. Heretofore repressed desires now grew into glorious and challenging philosophies." Here, looking straight into the eyes of the audience, I asked in a ringing voice: "And do you know how these yearnings impressed the tender soul of the young poet?"

There was a silence like the silence in a shul during the "Eighteen Blessings." But before I could answer my question, there was a loud voice from the first row: "I have no idea."

The voice came from an elderly man. He had a tiny face full of wrinkles, a dense cluster of peppery hair and he wore wire-rimmed glasses tied around his ears with black shoestrings. Who was he? A jester? A saboteur? A moron? I thought that the best thing would be to ignore him. Which I did.

I proceeded with the lecture exalted and drunk with my own words. "Leywick," I said, "was not only our spiritual messenger who carried in himself the dreams and cravings of every single individual, he was also our folk-poet, who carried the dreams of the whole Jewish nation." Here I paused and asked dramatically: "How could he at the same time be both our personal as well as our national bard?"

"I can't imagine," said the little guy in the wire-rimmed glasses.

I gave him a sharp look. He sat there with the face of an innocent suckling. There was nothing to do but to proceed with the talk. I quoted a number of Leywick's lines and illustrated some of my contentions with complete stanzas. I analyzed their rhythms, assonances, meters, accentuations and ictuses. All the arguments till now were a preparation for the ultimate attempt to answer the age-old query: What is it that makes a Jewish poet Jewish? I started with an enigmatic statement: "For a Jewish poet to be totally Jewish he must possess four qualities. And Leywick possessed them all. His poetry contains the element of messianism; it has the simultaneous presence of belief and doubt; it possesses the subject of suffering. . . . And do you know"—here I took the pose of Cicero—"what the fourth indispensable element is?"

"No," said the bespectacled little monster and for the first time there was a ripple of giggles from the public.

Heroically I plodded along but my mood became darker and darker. The old freak with the guiltless expression on his face continued to kill each of my rhetorical questions. I managed within the next ten minutes to construct a new thesis about the ambiguity in Leywick's soul, about his concurrent longing and fear of the Messiah. "He at the same time possessed the vision of "somewhere far, somewhere far, lies the land of the forbidden . . . " but he also could see the nightmare of a Redeemer that may come around armed with a fist and an ax . . . " I stabbed my index finger towards heaven and asked in a reverberating voice: "So who, according to Leywick, was the veritable deliverer?"

"How should I know?" said the man with the wrinkled face and peppery chevelure.

I swiftly moved ahead to prevent the audience's chuckle from developing into an open outbreak of laughter. I embarked on the theme of Leywick's rebellions against God. I quoted poems of outright mutiny against God's injustices, showing that his faith was based not on flattery or humility but on daring and defiance. I quoted the flaming words: "My powerlessness cries out to you, to you who are everlasting and mighty; Night and day, day and night, I'm sick of always being righteous . . . " I finished off this section of the talk with a ringing question: "And what were the reasons that transformed Leywick's faith into this act of sedition?"

"The less I know, the less it'll hurt me," the man answered with an old Jewish idiom. It took the chairman a whole minute to silence the roaring audience.

YEHUDA HALEVI
AND GOLDA

The people were already in their seats and I was ready to walk up to the lectern, but the chairman, a short and puffy gentleman with a bald head took me gently by an elbow and led me into an adjacent room.

"Mr. Schultz," he said, "there is a little matter we have to discuss before you begin."

I apologetically stated that my name was not Schultz, but he waved it away as irrelevant.

"We know, of course," he said, "that the subject of your lecture is our great national poet Yehuda Halevi. However, I was instructed by the executive to ask you to make the lecture more timely."

I said: "I'm afraid I don't understand."

"This is," he said, "what I am about to clarify. We would like you to combine the subject of your lecture with the latest events in Israel."

"You must be joking," I said.

"I'm a hundred percent serious. Ordinarily a subject like Yehuda Halevi would be sufficient in itself, but considering the important thing going on in the Middle East, it would be an error to leave this all out."

"Mr. Chairman," I said. "Yehuda Halevi lived in Spain

in the second half of the sixteenth century and all I intend to do is to give an analysis of his works against the background of his times."

"Analyze it as much as you like," said the chairman, "but find an episode in his life which can give you an excuse to present a small briefing of the present situation in the Middle East."

"I don't see how a thing like this could be done."

"All we want you to do, Mr. Schultz, is to drop from time to time a name like Golda Meir, Moshe Dayan or Kurt Waldhein, and also one or two names of Arabs, then you could safely slip back to your subject and talk about Yehuda Halevi's poetry to your heart's desire."

"I'm sorry," I said, "this is absolutely unthinkable."

"You are going to be stubborn?" he asked.

"I'm not stubborn, but I see no way in which to drag Yehuda Halevi into the peace negotiations led by Gunnar Jarring."

The chairman gave me a sharp look which meant: "This is the last time your foot has stepped over our threshold." and he led me back into the hall. But there, at the very beginning of my lecture which I usually start with the words: "One of our greatest national poets, Yehuda Halevi . . . , " I said instead of Yehuda Halevi—"Golda Meir." The chairman glanced at me with delight and gave a sign to the audience to join him in frenetic applause.

AFFECTION FOR ISRAEL

After I finished a lecture to an organization, a pleasant young man came up to me with a request. Would I agree to give the same lecture to a group of young people who were organized in a younger set of the same organization? The members of the set, of which he was the chairman, are all young men and women with a very limited knowledge of Yiddish. But they feel a great affinity for this language and they have expressed a desire to listen to a talk in Yiddish. The only condition was that I should speak slowly. And another thing—with as few as possible Hebrew words.

The group indeed appeared to be most enthusiastic. The subject was "Jewish poetry between the two World Wars" and I tried to be as simple and accessible as possible. The young women and men who filled the room listened with acute attention. Everything seemed to be alright except for one thing. Somewhere, towards the middle of the talk, they suddenly broke out in loud frenetic applause. At first I was puzzled but when it happened again I quickly discovered the reason.

They clapped each time I mentioned the name of the well-known religious Jewish poet Israel Stern. Whenever I mentioned his name they thought that I was talking about the land of Israel and they very patriotically applauded.

After I finished, a young man at the executive table proposed that all those present should, as an expression of thanks to the speaker, buy more Israeli bonds.

A VERY SERIOUS CHAIRMAN

The subject was Shalom Aleychem. Every seat was occupied and people were dragging in additional chairs. The atmosphere was warm, the mood was cheerful, the audience was ready for a humorous excursion into the world of the shtetl, to spend the next hour in the company of such characters as Menachem Mendel, Tevye, the cantor's boy Motel, and even the old horse Methushelak. People were looking at me in advance, with smiling eyes and even with love. I knew the meaning of their smiles: they were intended not for me but for the greatest of all Jewish humorists whose name was synonymous with laughter, with mirth and with joy. "Laughter is healthy," said the master, and the audience came for a delightful medical treatment. I felt exceptionally pleased being the one to deliver the cure.

But there was an exception to the rule and the exception was the chairman. He was a middle-aged man with dense bushy eyebrows and the nose of an albatross. While everyone around was smiling and ready to burst into laughter, he was as cloudy as the top of a skyscraper on a foggy day. He performed the introductory formalities in a somber voice, then pushed the mike to me and gave me a sign to start.

As soon as I got up the audience began to clap; this was a down payment for the applause I was to receive later. But at that instant the chairman sprang to his feet, pulled the mike to himself and said in a firm voice:

"Ladies and Gentlemen, I must insist on a civilized behavior. Please refrain from any demonstrations and disturbances."

His announcement came to me as a surprise. What sort of disturbance was this wave of friendly clapping? But the listeners knew him better: from that moment on everybody sat quietly, frozen to his seat.

I spoke with verve about Kasrylevke, the characters of Yehupetz, Tevye's daughters, and quoted passages of the most humorous monologues. All this time the chairman remained stiff on his chair, his albatross nose thrust forward, his rapacious eyes piercing the audience who didn't dare budge. Only once, while I read one of the most hilarious letters of Menachem Mendel to his wife Sheyne Shayndel, one of the men in the audience could stand it no longer and began shaking with laughter. The chairman got up, looked at the culprit and said in a soft but murderous voice: "Mr. Birenbaum, if you want to laugh, you may go home. There you may roar like a wild donkey. Not here. This is a cultural institution."

Mr. Birenbaum blushed and hung his head. I intended to go on, but the chairman wasn't finished; he had a message not only to Mr. Birenbaum but to the rest of the assembly: "I'd like to draw everyone's attention to the fact that we aren't in a circus. If anybody plans to behave in a way which doesn't befit the character of this evening, he can take his wife and go home."

Why he had to send along his wife, I couldn't figure out. Never did I have such an audience during a lecture on Shalom Aleykhem. I told them the best parts of Kasrylevke, the spiciest dialogues of the Stories of a Salesman, I quoted the rhymed curses of Shalom Aleykhem's step-mother—to no avail. They sat till the end like a shul during Kol Nidrey on Yom Kippur. When I finished with Shalom Aleykhem's saying: "Laughter is healthy," the chairman gave me a dirty look. There was no applause. The chairman himself clapped once and immediately announced "question time." The only question came from an elderly lady who asked in a dark voice: "Of what disease did Shalom Aleykhem die?" I told her: "Of tuberculosis." The public got up and left in grave silence. While I put my coat on the chairman came over, shook my hand and said solemnly: "Our audience may not be big, but you must admit that it's well-mannered."

I admitted.

A TELEVISION INTERVIEW IN MEXICO

I was ready to start out on a new lecture tour in the South when the chief lecture organizer of the New York office had a splendid idea: why shouldn't I, being so close to the Mexican border, take advantage, get on a plane and give one or two lectures to the Yiddish speaking Jewish audiences in Mexico City?

He called the leaders of the fraternal Jewish organization in the Mexican capital and they responded with an enthusiasm that surpassed my own expectations. Not only would they organize two lectures in one of Mexico's central lecture halls, they would arrange for me as well an interview on one of the local television stations. This would be, they said, the first time in the history of the Mexican television, that the Spanish viewers will see a Jewish speaker and listen to the Yiddish tongue.

At first the idea frightened me; I foresaw a whole lot of complications, but I was soon told, in a following letter, that the arrangement was to be very simple: the whole interview will consist of exactly twelve questions and answers. All I'm expected to do is to stand in front of the camera, face the interviewer and reply, in a prearranged order, to his Spanish questions with my Yiddish answers.

In other words, without understanding a word of Spanish and him not understanding a word of Yiddish, the interview will run as smoothly as silk. At the end the Spanish man will finish up with a brief summary of my twelve replies.

It all sounded perfectly simple and I stopped worrying.

As soon as I arrived in Mexico City I was given a sheet containing the twelve questions marked with Roman numerals like the Ten Commandments. The questions were easy, the answers were easy, everything looked dandy.

The interview was to take place the next day, on a Sunday, at two in the afternoon. An hour earlier the leader of the Mexican Jewish Kehilla himself showed up at my hotel in his limousine and we drove to the TV station in one of the suburbs of that gigantic city. I came excellently equipped. I knew all the questions by rote. I could recite them from top to bottom, bottom to top and sideways. The first of my interview questions would be: "How many Jews live in the United States of America?" I would reply briefly and to the point: "The USA has a population of over five and a half million Jews. Most of them live in the big cities." The first question would be followed by the second: "How many American Jews speak Yiddish?" And so on—up to number twelve.

We arrived at the studio at a quarter to two. A young Mexican woman made me sit in front of a mirror and began putting makeup on my face. While the young señorita was busy transforming me into a glamor boy, I kept repeating in a subvocal voice and for the last time the twelve ominous questions with their twin replies.

A minute later I was led into a room where I settled comfortably into a leather upholstered armchair fronting a row of flashlights. A second later the interviewer entered, a young, handsome Mexican who looked like a grandson of Montezuma. We shook hands. He said "Buenas dias" and I replied, good-humoredly, "Shalom Aleichem." The lights went on, the cameras began rolling and my Mexican interviewer introduced the program by saying to the viewers a few enthusiastic words about today's guest. The only word that I did understand was, of course, my name, which sounded on his lips like the name of an Aztec deity.

He then gave me a sign that he was ready and I changed into a pair of earphones. Alas, instead of beginning directly with the question number one ("How many Jews live in the USA?") he considered it his duty to begin with an additional act of courtesy by saying to me in a reverberating voice: "I welcome you, my dear sir, on your visit to our country."

Being convinced that he had, according to our worked out strategy, given me the first question, I shot back the response number one. As a result of this tiny misunderstanding, the interview went on like this:

He: I Welcome You, my dear sir, on your visit to our country.

I: The United States of America has a population of over five and half million Jews. Most of them live in the big cities.

He: How many Jews are there in the United States of America?

I: Some of them speak Yiddish, but the overwhelming majority speak English.

ue: Do the American Jews speak Yiddish?

I: The largest Yiddish newspaper in the USA is the Jewish Daily Forward.

He: What is the largest Yiddish newspaper in the USA?

I: It is called "Folksbiene" and is run by the Workmen's Circle.

He: Does New York have a Yiddish theater?

I: Yes, the Yiddish writers are organized into a group which is a part of the International Pen-Club.

He: Do the Yiddish writers belong to the International Pen-Club?

I: Oh, yes, the American Jews have a great interest in Israel.

He: Do the American Jews have an interest in Israel?

I: Two Yiddish writers have become famous to non-Yiddish readers. Elie Wiesel and Isaac Bashevis Singer.

He: Are there any Yiddish writers who have become known to non-Yiddish readers?

I: Yes, the Workmen's Circle has a medical department.

He: You mentioned earlier the Workmen's Circle. Does this organization have a medical department?

I: Some colleges have recently introduced Yiddish as a credit subject.

He: Is Yiddish being taught in American colleges?

I: This I don't know.

He: Do you know how many Russian Jews have lately come to the USA?

I: I have a wife and two children.

He: Excuse me for asking this: are you a family man, señor Shulman?

I: Another two days.

He: How long do you intend to stay in Mexico?

He seemed suprised when I looked at him blankly and said nothing. This was the moment when I realized that something had gone wrong. He quickly shook my hand, said a hasty "hasta luego," then the lights went out and the young and confused Montezuma vanished.

My friend, the leader of the Kehilla in Mexico City, had all this time been waiting in an adjacent room watching the show on a small screen. His face was as white as a sheet.

Directly from the studio we drove, without exchanging a word, to the lecture hall, which had already begun to fill up with people; all had watched the interview and they looked like ghosts.

Fortunately, the subject of my lecture was "The Murder of the Yiddish Culture in the Soviet Union." And soon everyone's mind was directed toward another calamity.

FUNERAL ORATIONS

I once more checked the obituary in the Yiddish newspaper and memorized the time of the service and the address of the funeral parlor. This was the first time I was asked to speak at a funeral and I was nervous.

The deceased was a distinguished Yiddish poet. A special committee was formed to organize the funeral, and appointed no less than six speakers to deliver the eulogies. The other five were themselves distinguished poets and close friends of the departed. The reason I was invited to be speaker number six was the fact that I had only recently arrived from France and that my presence would "symbolize the cosmopolitan character of Yiddish literature."

The ceremony was to take place in a funeral chapel in the upper part of West Side Manhattan. I arrived in time, clasping in my hand the speech which I had written down in printed letters. The hall was filled with a huge crowd. All the benches were occupied, people were standing in the aisles, along the walls and in the lobby outside the opened doors.

I sat with a pounding heart at the extreme end of the platform. Before mounting the platform we had all been advised as to the sequence of the speeches; I was, of course, speaker number six. I sat in silence, my heart hammering, listening to the eulogies of my five elder colleagues.

Each of them spoke about the importance of poetry in general, of the special importance of poetry in the life of the Jewish nation and of the particular role played by the deceased who occupied the "Eastern Wall in the Poetical Temple." Each of the five men illustrated his words with samples of the poet's verses. Some of them, profiting from the occasion, smuggled in lines of their own poetry.

The speeches were long and the people gathered in the hall began showing signs of restlessness.

After the five men had finished I got up from my seat and read in a nervous voice the very brief text of my own prepared speech. As soon as I pronounced the last word, the manager of the funeral parlor impatiently signaled his assistants, two tall men in tuxedoes and white shirts, who began carrying out the casket to the limousine waiting in the street.

As I was descending the platform, I was surrounded by three elderly ladies. Dressed in black costumes and wearing little round hats they looked like the Chekhovian Sisters. One of them smiled at me very charmingly and said: "Bravo! You stole the show." I looked back with puzzlement. Did I hear correctly? "She is right," said the other, "It was a pleasure listening to you." And the third lady rounded it up: "Hadn't it been for you, the whole thing would end up a flop."

It so happened that only a week later I was asked to deliver a speech at another funeral. This time the deceased was a well-known Jewish labor figure and socialist, and the chairman of the organization of which I was a member. It was on behalf of this organization that I had to deliver an eulogy.

The ceremony took place in a funeral chapel in Brooklyn. The street outside the building and the lobby were full of people, some of whom I knew. We greeted in silence with that philosophical nod which contained more pity for oneself than regret for the deceased.

I mounted the wide stairs and entered a narrow hall. I expected, as I knew from a similar previous case that the ceremony would be socialist in form and atheist in content, that the departed would not only listen to eulogies with praise, but also to revolutionary songs.

An open door in the corridor led to a packed room and when I tried to get in I was stopped by a tall broad shouldered young man. "Let me in," I said, "I'm one of the speakers." Hearing this the man took me firmly by an arm and pushing himself with force through the dense crowd, succeeded in dragging me to the opposite end of the hall where I mounted the platform.

As soon as I sat on the chair behind the table, someone next to me handed me a black satin yarmulkah and signaled me to put it right away on my bare head. I was stunned. I expected it to be not only a secular but a socialist ceremony where a yarmulkah is absolutely not kosher. Turning my head I glanced at the other speakers and was outright shocked. In the center of the platform, a few inches from the mike, sat an old man with a white chassidic beard. And likewise the others. Each one of them had a beard of a different size. I was the only one with a naked and shaved face.

I fell back in the chair and stared at the crowd in the hall and whispered to myself: "Mon Dieu!" (I was still in the habit of whispering to myself in French). All the men gathered in the hall wore skullcaps or black hats with wide rims and the ladies' heads were covered with black shawls.

I whispered again, this time a little louder: "Mon Dieu!" Was it possible that the deceased had, a few days before passing away, changed his convictions and left a will requiring a religious funeral? And if so, how was it possible that his lifelong comrades—all unbent socialists and anarchists—had overnight grown beards and renounced their allegiance to Marx and Kropotkin?

The most simple explanation would, of course, be that I had mistaken the room. But this didn't dawn upon me. I was still a recently arrived European and I didn't know of the existence of such wholesale funeral departments, where several different funerals took place at the same time in each room of the building.

Fortunately, my mistake had been noticed by others. A hand from behind suddenly grabbed me by the collar, pulled me down from the platform and dragged me through the hall, straight to the lobby. There a young man exclaimed joyfully: "Here you are!" He took me by an arm, helped me descend the stairs and we entered another room. Here everything was as I expected: the tribune was decorated with a red flag on which two brotherly hands were clasped in a sign of proletarian solidarity. The people in the benches sat bareheaded, red roses in their lapels. I mounted the platform at the moment one of the speakers finished off his speech with the phrase: "Workers of all countries, unite."

SOUTHERN HOSPITALITY

It was in Mississippi that I found out that the word "hospitality" isn't only linked to the word "hospital" linguistically.

A most charming elderly couple came up to me after my lecture and offered to come to my hotel the next morning and show me their beautiful city. They arrived with great punctuality, the little white haired lady sitting at the wheel of a magnificent limousine. Her husband sat in the back and invited me to sit beside him. I had come to this Mississippi city the previous afternoon and had no more than a superficial glimpse of the skyline; now I had the opportunity to see the city in all its glory.

We began by riding along wide tree-shaded avenues and parks. I wanted to tell this amicable courteous couple of my preference for museums and churches, but I decided to leave the choice to them.

Our first stop was before a tall building of black marble, amid trees and beds of flowers.

"This," said my host, "is the St. Gilbert Protestant Hospital. Only a few years ago it had six stories and only 120 beds; now the number of stories is doubled and the number of beds has more than tripled."

"This is our main hospital for lung diseases," added the little lady.

I looked up and subvocally counted the floors: there were twelve. I said "wonderful" and we drove on.

Our next stop was a building of white stone.

"St. Mary Hospital," announced the man, "Catholic."

He pointed to the left wing of the building. "This side is for the patients." He shifted his arm to the right: "This is where the laboratories are." "Kidneys," added the little woman, meaning that this was the place where they treated kidney diseases.

"Pity," said the man, "that these aren't visiting hours; we could have shown you the artificial kidneys."

The next building was right across the street, a cream painted edifice of square rocks. Before my host's announcement, I read aloud the golden letters on a black block of marble: Heart Diseases.

"Here," said the man, "people come not only from this state, but from all of North America."

"Even from Mexico," said his wife.

"Mexico is also in North America," he corrected.

The woman nodded: "Two of my sisters were treated in this hospital. One of them was cured."

"I'm sorry to hear that," I said. Both looked at me with surprise and I quickly added: "I mean about the one that wasn't."

We rode along a wide street full of trees, shrubs and fountains. We were passing a pink structure with tall columns.

"What hospital is that?" I asked.

"It isn't a hospital," the man said. "It's the Municipal Museum."

I suggested: "Could we stop for a while and visit it?"

The man looked at his watch and shook his head: "If we

stop here we'll miss the visiting hours of the hospital for arthritic diseases."

"Ten years ago," said the little woman, when we stopped before the building for arthritis, "our city was sending all our arthritic cases to Houston, Texas. Now, since this hospital was finished, not only are we not sending them to Texas any more, but I'm proud to say that Texas is sending their disabled to us."

The door of the hospital was open and a crowd was streaming into a huge lobby.

"Which would you prefer," the little woman asked, "to visit the top floors with the patients confined to their beds, or see the lower floors where the patients are able to move in invalid chairs or on crutches?"

I chose the crutches.

We spent half an hour there and then proceeded further. The woman pressed the gas.

"Don't rush, dear," said her husband, "or we may have an accident."

"This would be the right place for an accident," the woman said with humor, "for we're approaching the hospital for bone surgery."

I said: "You seem to have a great number of hospitals in this city."

"You haven't seen nothing," said the man. We stopped before the next: "Contagious diseases."

"If you show your presscard," said the man, "they may let you in."

I told him that I had left the card in the hotel and we drove on. The woman suddenly stopped in the middle of a street with no hospital in sight.

"Why did you stop?" asked the husband.

"I'm not sure what to do," said the woman. "Should we go next to the hospital for eye diseases or nose-ear-and-throat?"

"Let's ask Mr. Shulman," suggested the man.

"Nose-ear-and-throat," I said.

This was the last hospital we visited before noon. The next stop was a restaurant which had an exquisite menu. While I was selecting the items I heard the couple making plans for the afternoon: tumors, swellings, blood diseases, bladders. I put away the menu and said in a weak voice that I wasn't feeling well and that I wished to return to the hotel.

"Why the hotel?" asked the man, "why not a hospital?"

"You can have your pick," suggested the woman.

But I insisted. Despite the fact that I thanked them profusely, they left disappointed.

A SINGER
WHO LOST HIS VOICE

Audiences who are exposed to a lecture receive their compensation afterwards in the form of entertainment. The talk is followed by a brief interval during which the public is treated to coffee and homemade cookies, provided by one of the ladies. Then follows the real attraction: the artistic part.

The idea behind this arrangement is of a humanitarian nature. After an hour long lecture the public deserves a reward which comes either in the person of a singer, actor or musician. Very often the artist—like the previously served cookies—is home produced. Each social group has in its midst a talented lady who can sing a "bintel" of Yiddish folksongs, a "recitator" who knows a few Jewish poems by heart, an amateur comedian who has a memory for jokes and humorous monologues, or—in some instances—an elderly member who can play on a comb. It may also happen that one of the members will bring a three- or four-year-old grandchild prodigy, who can sing the entire "Star Spangled Banner" or the "Hatikvah."

But in most occasions the artist is a professional man or woman, who was hired by the executive board for a fee which is always higher than the speaker's fee. On several occasions it was suggested to me by the treasurer that I should give up a part of my pay so that my lecture could be "embellished by a real artist." The quality of the artist is always adapted to the quality of the speaker. A prominent and respected speaker gets a prominent and respected artist. A lesser speaker gets a lesser artist and a not so important speaker gets a home-taught or an amateur monologuist.

And another thing: the category of the speech must harmonize with the category of the artistic performance. A speaker who gives a lecture on Shalom Aleychem, will get an artist who will sing or play cheerful tunes. A somber speaker will get a moaning singer or a wailing actor.

However to every rule there are exceptions. And so it happened that after one of my lectures on Jewish humor, a lady with a dark voice recited: "The City of the Slaughterers," by the poet Ch. N. Bialik. And once, after a talk about the "Literature of Destruction," an actor from a Second Avenue Theatre told the public a few dozen blue jokes.

The professional artists are of various types and grades. The majority are singers. The men, fewer in number, are of the elderly type. In the males, the white haired or bald skulled is more respected than the young. Not so with the ladies, who should be younger and prettier. The result is that while male singers may grow in dignity with age, their female counterparts must, after reaching the age of dignity, step aside and be replaced by the newer and younger, who mostly come from Israel. For although the cultural work of these organizations is conducted strictly in Yiddish it is not a hindrance, nay, it's even a virtue, to have half of the artistic part executed in Ivrit. But for such a young Israeli crooner to satisfy the audience, she must (even if she is Iraqi or Yemenite) learn to sing "Mine Yiddish momme," or "Bei mir bistu sheyn."

The idea of the artistic part, as I mentioned before, is to give the audience a chance to forget the ordeal of the speaker. Unfortunately, the artistic part itself may prove to be an additional ordeal, for most of the singers, the men in particular, have a habit of delivering their own speeches. It is the prevailing custom that no self-respecting singer will simply announce the name of a song and immediately proceed to sing it. The singers, too, are men and women of intellect and they too have to say something to the audience.

In some cases they talk about the author of the lyrics, explain the content of the song and tell a few anecdotes about the composer. In other cases the singer may add personal reminiscences. This will take him back to the home of his parents, or grandparents, or to the shtetl. The latter may stimulate the artist to dwell a little longer on the subject of the Jewish shtetl in general and of his own shtetl in particular. He then gives a few thoughts on the influence the shtetl in Eastern Europe had on Jewish history, political movements and literature. Such an introduction to a song can in itself become a little lecture. If he is going to sing six songs, the audience would then listen to six such miniature speeches.

My own career was dotted with such a variety of artistic craftsmen, beginning from amateurish housewives, through professional debutants, until, as soon as my stature began to grow, my partners were the giants of the entertaining profession. One of them, a very much acclaimed and respected veteran of Yiddish folksongs, was my partner on the third or fourth year of my orational climbing. This was my first confrontation with a singer who spent half of his time delivering speeches.

I'll never forget how he appeared that time in a tuxedo, an impressively embroidered shirt and magnificent tie. He bowed very low and immediately announced the title of

124

his first song: "Three Little Daughters." I was sure that his pianist, an equally elderly gentleman with a naked skull, would instantly hit the keys; but the pianist knew better than this, for he continued reading his newspaper, while the singer proceeded to deliver a little lecture on the paradox of having daughters. On the one hand, he mused, all parents want their daughters to get married as soon as possible, while on the other hand, they live in fear that after their daughter's weddings the house will become sad and empty.

The singer quoted many examples of his own family which appeared to be large and endowed with a great number of girls. He underlined the existing difference between the family attachment to daughters among Jews and non-Jews, and after dwelling some time on the peculiarities of Jewish family life in Eastern Europe he went over to the undergone changes in Jewish family life in the United States. At this point he signaled the pianist, who put away his newspaper and began to play.

But he only placed it on the top of the piano, within reach, for each time the singer finished a song and started on a new speech, the pianist returned to his newspaper.

I had the opportunity of having the same singer several years later. It appeared that during these few years he had made remarkable progress, not with his singing but with his art of speech making.

He had recently come back from a trip to Israel and he gave the public a list of detailed impressions. The pianist wasn't at the piano, he was sitting in an adjoining room listening to a transistor radio. The singer compared his present trip to the Holy Land to a few of his previous trips. He was well acquainted with the Bible, he had not simply toured Israel, but he had followed in the footsteps of the biblical characters. He had already covered the paths of Abraham, Isaac, Jacob and the Twelve Tribes. His latest

125

trip took him on the roads of the Kings and some of the Prophets.

While he was talking the pianist had stuck his head in two or three times but quickly withdrew it and returned to his radio. Still floating on the wings of his reminiscences the singer didn't forget to make a few political comments: he praised Golda Meir, paid tribute to Moyshe Dayan, threw a few curses on the heads of the Arab oil lords in the Persian Gulf and expressed gratitude to the American government for its military help.

He finally exhausted the subject of Israel and embarked on his program. It appeared that he wasn't going to sing any songs from Israel—he was no longer of an age when it is easy to learn new texts—he announced the well-known "Three Little Daughters," which was the backbone of his repertoire. He began his introduction about the paradox of having daughters. No one listened, they all knew it by heart from other occasions. When he finished, the pianist shut off his radio, walked over to the piano and struck a few chords. The singer opened his mouth—but nothing came out. The pianist again hit the keys. The singer once more opened his mouth with the same result. The pianist who didn't seem to be surprised struck the keys for the third time, this time something did come out from the singer's throat, but it was scratchy and hoarse. It was clear that the long speech about Israel and then about the paradox of having daughters had taken away all his strength and his voice was gone.

But the public was sympathetic. Everybody stood up and began singing the song: "The Three Little Daughters." The singer was in no position to sing, but he waved his arms like a conductor. After this community singing was finished everybody clapped heartily and the singer bowed deeper than before. Everybody now sat down and the singer, with a hardly audible voice, announced that he was now going to sing "My Friend Yankele." As soon as he started the introduction about the importance of friendship among Jewish people, the pianist slipped to the adjoining room and turned on his transistor radio.

THE BUTTON

Hotel rooms play an important role in the business of lectures. A bright room may add to the lecture's brightness, somber rooms may introduce shadows of pessimism. The important thing is for the atmosphere of the room to be harmonious with the spirit of the talk.

This time the harmony was there. I was to lecture on my favorite poet, I. L. Peretz, who was elegant, sparkling and original. So was the room reserved by the executive. It was bright, furnished with cheerful furniture, golden lamps, a big brightly painted Utrillo on the wall, a color TV and a host of gadgets: a switch to boil coffee, another one to shine shoes and still another contraption to iron trousers. The desk drawers were filled with writing material, envelopes, pens and a leatherbound Bible. Dominating the room was a king-sized bed with enough space for our ancestor Jacob together with the twelve tribes.

Two hours before the lecture, the secretary of the organization called to see if everything was O.K. "Everything," I said, "is O.K." Should he come and pick me up half an hour earlier?" No, thank you very much." The hall was a few blocks away and I'd walk there myself. Half an hour before the lecture I started to get ready. I put on my white shirt, purple tie, black suit, put a handkerchief in my breast pocket and stood before the gold-framed mirror.

Everything was perfect. Except that the jacket button was hanging loosely by one thread.

It was a single-breasted suit and this button kept the two lapels together. When I touched the button to probe the strength of the thread, it flipped and fell into my hand. I knew that half an hour from now I'd be standing on a podium and that the eyes of the audience would be concentrated on no one else but me. It was unthinkable that I should stand there with my lapels flying like two sails of a boat and that my tie should flick around like the tail of an unruly horse.

I also knew that whatever the quality of the lecture, the richness of thought and opulence of content, the listeners wouldn't notice. Instead they would look at the point where my coat ends should be kept together by the unifying button, but where now they would let the tie roam around like a drunken wino.

I looked at my watch and knew that I must quickly find a way to attach the button to the jacket. I started feverishly to open all the desk drawers although I knew what little chance there was to find a needle and still less a spool of thread. I ran into the white glittering bathroom: could the button be glued on with soap? I ran back to the room, looked at every piece of furniture, scanned the surface of the walls, until my eyes stopped suddenly on the picture of the French painter Maurice Utrillo. There I saw my deliverance.

The painting was suspended from a thin nail and I had an inspirational thought: Who said that a button must be fastened with a thread only? I swiftly took down the painting and pulled the nail out of the wall with my bare fingers. The nail was thin, which was good, but it was long, which wasn't so good. However, under the circumstances there was no point in looking for perfection.

I took off the jacket, laid it on the desk, put the button at the exact spot where it belonged, placed the point of the nail in the buttonhole and began to hammer it in with my hairbrush. The nail was smooth and slim; it slipped easily into the buttonhole and went through the lapel of the coat.

I again put on the coat and stood before the mirror. Wonderful! I smoothed my tie for the last time and checked the handkerchief in my breast pocket.

Twenty minutes later the chairman made the formal introduction addressing the gathered men and women: "My dear friends . . . "

I announced the name of the lecture: "I. L. Peretz—our great classic." At the word classic I felt a delicate scratch on my chest. The point of the nail had evidently slipped through my shirt.

The scratch wasn't dangerous but it was a signal that in case of a more violent move it could penetrate my flesh and reach the muscle of my heart. For the first time in the history of Jewish lecturers one of them would suddenly exclaim "Shema Israel" and roll down to the feet of the people sitting in the first row.

The probability of such a violent move was very real. I.L. Peretz is one of the poets who uses an abundance of invocations, rhetorical questions and exclamations. Speakers who have ever talked on this subject are well aware how hard it is to remain motionless while quoting from his works. I therefore decided to quote as little as possible and remain as stiff as a marble statue. But taking such a resolution underestimated the power of the great bard.

One of the famous Peretzian tales is the story of a man who doubted the rumors spread by a rabbi's chasidim that the holy man spends every night in heaven. In order to prove that the rumors were a lie, he hid under the rabbi's bed. As soon as everybody in the house was asleep, he saw, to his amazement, that the rabbi got up from bed, put on the clothes of a woodchopper, went stealthily to the forest, chopped up a bundle of wood and carried it to the house of a poor and sick widow. Next morning, when the chasidim asked the doubting man: "Well, did the rabbi go to heaven?" The man replied: "If not higher." When I came to the end of the story and exclaimed "if not higher," I felt another scratch with the nail, a little more painful than before. And when I recited the poem: "Oh, different would sound my singing," the point of the nail must have pierced the texture of the shirt and got to the skin.

I now came closer to Peretz's masterpiece, "The Golden Chain," which contains the famous exclamation: "Let it be Shabbath" followed by the lines: "And so we are marching, singing and dancing . . . " I knew that here the nail may glide between my ribs; and that here I shall grab the mike and, together with the speaker's lectern, tumble to the floor.

I could no longer think of the elegance of the lecture or the opulence of its thoughts. All I was concerned with now was how to save the remaining few years of my life. A fortunate thought came to me when I arrived at the drama "At Night in the Old Market Place" which has a jester's monologue. This gave me the idea to stand in the pose of a clown, put a hand behind my lapel and, while reciting the lines, start pushing back the perilous nail. At first it wouldn't budge, but then it suddenly changed its mind and began to slip forward, threatening to fall out altogether, which would cause the button (I was now reciting the beautiful "Hope and Believe") to drop to the floor.

This same poem gave me the simultaneous opportunity to put a hand on my breast and push the nail back to its original position.

The final mortal risk was the poet's admonition: "Oh, don't think that the whole world is a pub!" I always use

THE FRIENDLY COUPLE
FROM THE BRONX

I looked at the invitation again and found the secretary's telephone number. I called him up.

—Mr. Berenholtz?

—Yes.

—The secretary of the Cultural Circle?

—Yes.

—I'm tonight's lecturer. I don't know your neighborhood and I don't think I'll be able to find your place.

He thought for a moment.

—Are you sure?

—I'm positive. I know how to get to the subway station, but I don't know your neighborhood.

—You said that before.

—Yes, I did.

—Suppose you ask someone when you get off the subway?

—I thought about that. But suppose they don't know either?

—What about asking a policeman?

—It may be hard to find one. You know how they are.

—What about the token-booth attendant?

—He may not know either.

There was another brief silence as Mr. Berenholtz thought:

133

—In that case there's only one solution.
—Which is?
—I'll wait for you at the station myself.
—I'll be very grateful.
—I'll pick you up at the exit.
—You're very kind.
—However, there is a slight problem.
—For instance?
—We don't know each other.
—That's true.
—We have never had the pleasure.
—True again.
—But the problem can be easily solved.
—Yes?
—I'll hold a copy of the Jewish Daily Forward.
—Excellent.

We agreed to meet at six thirty. I thanked him very much and he said that I was welcome.

I live at the opposite end of New York, in Sea Gate, Brooklyn, and it took about about two hours until my train pulled into the Bronx station at a quarter past six. It was the rush hour and the crowd was large. The stairs leading up to the street were crammed with people hurrying up and down with the usual lack of concern for their neighbors. A tall guy with sharp elbows and wire-rimmed glasses saddled on a conspicuous nose stepped rudely on my foot and subsequently gave me a push which knocked off my hat. Even if he didn't do it on purpose he demonstrated an unforgivable clumsiness. Looking straight into his eyes I loudly proclaimed: "Savage Hottentot." His eyes turned into two cups of venom and he retaliated: "Lumbering moron."

I'm not a wrangler, I'd rather suffer an injustice than get involved in a brawl; but this fellow irked me (perhaps because he towered me by at least a foot). I replied with a strongly accentuated tri-syllable: "Idiot." This evoked an instant answer from the region of zoology: "Rhinoceros," to which he quickly added: "Dinosaur."

In the meantime I managed to pick up my hat, and the sight of it, covered with dust, made me turn back to the man with the sharp cheekbones and say introducing a new angle: "Racketeer."

This onomatopoeic exchange of epithets was only between myself and the arrogant fellow with the pointed elbows. But after my "racketeer" a third person appeared on the stage and transformed us into a trio. This was a short and hefty woman wearing a hat made of plastic gardenias. She said to the man with the wire-rimmed glasses: "Why do you let this hooligan offend you?"

Spurred on by this new stimulus, he gave me a fresh murderous look and said, somewhat unexpectedly: "Bloody bastard." To which the little woman with the gardenia added: "Cutthroat." Now I had to carry the struggle on a double front. I could throw one insult at a time to each of the parties, but I selected a collective word which would embrace them both at the same time: "Cattle."

With that I turned away, convinced that this last collective expression had ended the dispute. But they wouldn't let me have the triumph of the last word. The tall fellow with the Mongolian cheekbones threw a brief one syllable "Bum" after me; while the woman, not exhausted by the incident, rounded it up with "Lumbering swine," "insolent pig" and "foul imbecile."

I was shaking all over when I reached the street. It was twenty after six. I walked into a cafeteria and asked for a Seven-up. I still could feel the burning insults of this horrible couple and also felt low because of my own vulgarity. I gulped down the Seven-up and followed it with a chaser: an ice cold Pepsi. The two drinks did little to

135

lower the temperature of my mood. With nerves still trembling I started back toward the station to meet Mr. Berenholtz. My eyes were suddenly drawn to a copy of the Jewish Daily Forward, displayed in a man's hand.

I looked up. The owner of the hand was the tall guy with the hornrimmed glasses, Mr. Berenholtz. He was standing close to a short lady wearing a hat with plastic gardenias, Mrs. Berenholtz.

There's an old Yiddish saying: "I wish the earth would open and swallow me alive." But such miracles never happen. Instead, I walked up to the man with the Jewish Daily Forward and said sheepishly: "Mr. Berenholtz, I presume?"

Fortunately, both Mr. and Mrs. Berenholtz had a sense of humor. On the way to the lecture hall, Mr. Berenholtz said:

—Somehow I had a premonition that the man whose foot I stepped on was you.

—How come?—I asked.

Both looked at each other and Mrs. Berenholtz said: "You look like a shlimazel."

We marched cheerfully on.

A SYMPOSIUM

This wasn't an ordinary lecture but an event which in the lingo of Yiddish cultural activities is called a "symposium." There was little relation to the symposium of ancient Greece—no reclining chairs, no dancing, no music or exquisite food. The only similarity was that both had speeches.

The symposium was to deal with a very controversial matter: with the subject of Shalom Asch, one of the most prominent Yiddish writers who created, in the last years of his life, a great upheaval in the minds of his readers. His novels "The Nazarene," "The Apostle" and "Mary" were decried by a large number of his readers and critics as a call to apostasy, a temptation to embrace the Christian religion. His life, till the end of his days, was embittered by hostility, poisoned by aggressive articles and vicious pamphlets. Even later after he died this storm had not easily subsided. It was in the middle of this electrified atmosphere that a New York Jewish group organized this symposium. The subject had a provocative title "The Christian Teachings of Shalom Asch."

Two speakers were engaged—an accuser, who was to throw verbal slings and arrows at the writer, the other one was called to defend Shalom Asch. I was engaged to play the part of the moderator, to mitigate the two speakers, to blunt the edges of their addresses and at the end, to summarize and reconcile their arguments.

The three of us met the day before and we rehearsed our roles. The first to speak was the accuser. He had prepared a violent attack on the author of "The Nazarene" proving that Shalom Asch was a renegade and traitor to the Jewish people. The defender in return prepared a vitriolic attack against the first speaker pointing out that he knew nothing of the intricacies of literary art. Both had written down their speeches; the case was too serious to depend on memory.

The symposium drew a big crowd. Hundreds of men and women filled every seat in the hall of a midtown hotel. The public came even earlier than advertised, as did the executive and the second speaker—the defender. But not the accuser. A quarter of an hour after the announced time the telephone rang; the first speaker was on the other end and he announced in a desperate voice that he was still in the Bronx, that his subway train had broken down and that he didn't see how he would make it in less than an hour. He suggested that we would start the symposium with a changed order: let the other speaker talk first, while he would speak second.

The suggestion was logical and I notifed the second speaker of this unforseen happening. I told him that I was going to give my brief introduction after which he would get the floor. But he shook his head: this was impossible. He had prepared his speech in the form of an attack on the first speaker. He was going to tear apart everything the first speaker said, pointing out that he was a nobody, a peasant and a complete idiot; an ignoramus that never understood the deeper meaning of Shalom Asch's writing. How, then, could he throw all these amassed insults on the head of a man who hasn't yet shown up?

But the people in the hall began to get restless. The

138

program also included a folk singer, who was to provide the "artistic supplement;" but the singer was scheduled to arrive at the end of the symposium and we couldn't start the evening with his accompanying pianist, for he was a terrible musician. Neither could we start serving the coffee and danishes; first of all nobody has ever started a cultural evening with food; and secondly, everybody had just had supper at home.

I had a brief consultation with the chairman: even if the subway had been repaired by now, it would take our first speaker at least three quarters of an hour to arrive from the Bronx; it was impossible to wait that long. The people would simply get up, demand their money and leave. I explained this to the second speaker. I told him that there was no other way; he must speak first.

He again shook his head: no and no. But the chairman made a firm decision—he got up and announced that "The symposium is open." I went over to the mike and made a few introductory remarks on the subject of Shalom Asch, announced the change in the program (making a few sarcastic remarks about the New York Transit Authority) and called upon the second speaker.

He walked up to the lectern like a condemned man, pulled out his prepared speech from his breast pocket, and began to read. His first words were: "Mr. Chairman, Mr. Moderator, Ladies and Gentlemen. We have just listened to a terrible and preposterous attack against our beloved Shalom Asch . . . "

The people looked at each other in astonishment. What attack? The speaker himself stopped and looked at me with despair, but I motioned him to go ahead.

He started throwing the most violent and vile insults on the head of the first speaker (who was, at this moment stuck in the broken down subway). He raised his voice and proclaimed:

139

"The speaker we have just listened to, is an irresponsible individual; a man with not a trace of culture; he didn't understand a single word of Shalom Asch's writings. And why, ladies and gentlemen, didn't he? For the very plain reason that he is a brainless creature and a moronic ass."

The speaker gradually became heated up by his own words. He began to raise his voice and even to hit the lectern with a fist: "Shalom Asch is a literary giant," he shouted, "a genius among the greatest writers of the world; he also is a great and wonderful Jew. And who was the speaker who had the insolence to attack him? A narrow-minded nincompoop. No, not even narrow-minded, for he has no mind at all. He is a cretin. He is the embodiment of stupidity. Only a miserable idiot could talk like this about the greatest Jewish novelist, the author of the 'Tehilim Yid'."

The speaker became more and more agitated. He said that the "previous speaker" (who was still riding the Bronx subway) was a scoundrel and a gangster. He was worse than Torquemada of the Spanish Inquisition. Worse than Savonarola. He compared him to the pogromtchik Bogdan Chmielnitzki, to the Russian tsars, to the anti-Semites of the "Black Hundred" and even to Stalin.

Sitting in the center of the podium I could see that the people in the hall were also gradually beginning to get warmed up by the words of the speaker. They even started to applaud some of his more violent phrases. They clapped long and loud when he said "The previous speaker is a veritable hooligan who spilled the blood of our great Asch!"

The mood in the hall became one of great love to the wronged Jewish writer and terrible hatred to the speaker who hadn't arrived yet, much less opened his mouth.

When the speaker finished with the slogan: "Hands off our beloved Shalom Asch! Down with his attackers!"

everybody sprang to his feet and gave the speaker a tumultuous applause.

At this moment the door opened and the first speaker, after his ordeal in the subway, came in. He expected cheers, instead he was greeted with a dead silence and murderous looks. When I announced that he was going to speak, half the people got up and ran toward the door. The other half began to whistle, stamp their feet and shout: "Boo!"

A WOMAN WITH EARRINGS

A Jewish organization asked me to give a talk on the theme of "Isaac Bashevis Singer—his place in Jewish and world literature."

I arrived at the scheduled time, even though I knew that there's usually a chasm of one-and-a-half or even two hours between the scheduled time and the time when the lecture really begins.

When I entered the lecture room, there was no one there as yet, only a Puerto Rican woman mopping the floor. A bit later, the secretary showed up and began putting out the chairs. Next came the cashier: he set up a table at the entrance, laid out the tickets, and put down a wooden box for the dollar bills.

And shortly thereafter, someone else walked in, a woman wearing earrings.

There's nothing unusual about earrings, and it wouldn't ordinarily merit a story title. But there was nothing usual about these earrings.

The woman was still of a fairly acceptable age, that is to say, an age in which it was still important for her to emphasize that she's a woman. She was wearing a head of bought (or rented) hair terminating in two braids, one of which (the right one) was darker than the other. Her cheeks were rouged red, brick red, her lips were scarlet and her eyes had blue shadows under them and long false eyelashes.

She looked like Cleopatra of Ancient Egypt, or like Cecil B. DeMille's notion of Queen Vashti, or a Yiddish theater soubrette in the part of Auntie May from Bombay.

She was also wearing a bit of jewelry, not from New York's jewelry center on Forty-seventh Street, however, but from Greenwich Village. She had three or four strings of dried peas around her neck, a broach with the head of a green spider pinned onto the center of a sparsely buttoned blouse, and ten colored rings on all ten fingers, which terminated in blue-tinted nails.

Her principal adornments, however, were the earrings. They were big, round, flat brass plates reaching practically all the way to her elbows. They looked like two wheels of a Roman chariot, or like two cymbals of a Biblical orchestra playing in the Temple; or like two brass skillets on which our Jewish mothers used to fry scrambled eggs with onions.

She walked in with a loud cowboyish "HI!" to the cashier who was sitting by the door waiting for customers and zoomed straight towards me.

Then she halted about a yard away from me and started looking at me the way you look at an item in a department store when you intend to buy it. Now she moved closer, about half a yard away, screwed her right eye with the thick lashes, and extended a plump and energetic hand.

Observing the laws of etiquette, I held out my hand in return (my hand, of course, is slender and artistic); she clutched and tickled it with her fingers: "It's a great pleasure to meet you in the flesh."

I replied (according to the same code) that the pleasure was all mine, and I waited for further developments. And further developments came.

143

She came even closer (let's say about nine inches away from me), so close that I found myself swimming in a cloud of pungent perfumes (twenty-five cents a bottle). Again she screwed one eye (this time the left one) and slapped my shoulder: "Don't you want to know who I am?"

"Yes, who are you?"

But her question was merely a trap. She shot back with a loud, monosyllabic laugh: "Does it really make any difference to you? As long as I'm a female." She slapped my shoulder again. "You look like an innocent lamb."

She backed up and scrutinized me from top to bottom. "Just as I imagined you! You don't even look like you could count to ten, at least on the outside. But inside! Inside, there's a kettle of pitch boiling away."

The light from the chandelier reflected off her earrings, and the two cymbals blazed like fire.

She spoke no Yiddish, only Brooklynese English. She stood facing me with the two blazing earrings and scrutinized me for the second or third time. This time she screwed both eyes at once and, staring intently with two fiery eyes, shook her head: "I just don't understand how you do it."

—How I do—what?

—How do you get them?

—How do I get who?

—You know perfectly well who you get.—She ogled me again: You're not good-looking. You're not virile, you're not muscular. So why do they come running?

—Who?

—You know perfectly well who.

I didn't know. The whole thing was a puzzle. Who was she? What was she after? Certainly not the meager check I was getting for the lecture. I was standing with my back to the wall and I couldn't back off any more. And she was standing in front of me, exuding a ticklish cloud. One braid was thrown over her shoulder, the other hung down in front.

The spider on her broach had two green watery eyes, and both eyes looked at me with the same calculation as the two blue-circled eyes of the woman with the blazing earrings. I kept casting nervous glances at the secretary and the cashier, but they were busy with the audience which had begun arriving for the lecture.

The woman with the two brass plates also looked at the audience who were settling in the seats. She shook her head:

—Do you think I came to hear your lecture?

—No?

—I don't go to lectures. They're a waste of time. But you're a different matter entirely.

—Why am I a different matter?

—You intrigue me.

—How do I intrigue you?

—I'm curious about your power.

—What power?

—You know perfectly well what power.

—I don't know at all.

—I've made a list of all your conquered fortresses.

—What fortresses?

She came even closer. I was standing with my back to the wall, as I mentioned a moment ago, and there was no way I could move. I felt hot, and the heat smelled of cologne. She shook her head, and one of the brass plates swung dangerously close to my neck. She gave me another slap on the shoulder. And laughing with a dark laughter, she said: "I wouldn't care if I were a conquered fortress."

The puzzle became more and more obscure. Who was she? What did she want? What did her words mean? I'd never seen her before.

The auditorium was full. The chairs were all occupied.

145

The chairman, sitting behind the praesidium table, called out to me: "Comrade Shulman, we can start now."

I looked at him as at a Messiah. "Excuse me," I said to the woman, "they're calling me." She blocked my path.

—He's not calling you. He's calling someone named Shulman.

—That's me.

—You?

—Me.

She glared at me with two burning eyes: "You're not Isaac Bashevis Singer?"

She stormed over to the door and loudly asked the cashier to give her back her dollar. She whipped out of the room, and with her went the blazng glare of her two brass earrings.

The hall began to dim. A darkness descended that was just right for talking about devils, demons, goblins and gnomes.

ISAIAH—THE PROPHET, GIVES A LECTURE

It was a cold wintery evening when I boarded the bus to Montreal. Inside, it was deliciously warm and I thought with pleasure of the long and relaxing ride. The subject of the lecture I was to give the next day in Montreal was: "The Prophets and their Teachings." As soon as the bus began to roll, I put off the lights and I closed my eyes. I had a sudden thought: Here I was going to speak about the prophets, but what about the prophets themselves? How did they deliver their own speeches? Did they actually mount a platform near the central tower of a city and hold forth to a random crowd? Or were the addresses given in a formal fashion, in rented halls and in the manner familiar to us who attend organizational functions?

It must be obvious to those of us who believe that ancient times were much like modern times, that in Old Jerusalem, as in our New York, organizations existed which ran cultural activities, and, from time to time, in accordance with their budgetary capacities, invited the prophets to give lectures.

Each branch of the national organization must have received, at the beginning of the season, a brochure from the central office giving a list of speakers and themes which they dealt with.

No doubt among the most popular of speakers was Isaiah, the prophet who specialized in lyrical descriptions of his visions.

Daniel must have been a favorite too, especially among those who spoke Babylonian. Young people must have been entranced by his talk on lions' dens.

On solemn occasions Jeremiah must have been much sought after, especially when historic milestones were commemorated.

Another popular speaker must have been Jonah the Prophet, although the veracity of his account of being inside a big fish was somewhat suspect.

The lectures by the prophets were not, of course, independent programs. Each one was added to an important event involving the branch or some of its leaders, for example, as an added attraction when a couple celebrated their golden wedding anniversary, or when the grandson of the president was Bar Mitzvah, or when a reception was tendered to the secretary on his return from a trip to Egypt.

The lectures were a way of attracting more people to various simchas.

The guests were also invited to enhance the appearance of the dais. This made speakers adorned with patriarchal beards especially desirable. And the branches also needed the lectures so they could be cited in annual reports to the "national." This was an assurance that something cultural had been done, thus winning a subsidy from the central office.

Prophets were probably paid in accordance with the beauty of their beards. Those with long, imposing beards got higher fees than those with shorter ones. The important thing was not the content of the address but the quality of the beard.

But one thing must be said about the beards of that era;

they were genuine, unlike those sported by some latter-day lecturers who wear pasted on beards and sideburns.

The lectures were, of course, publicized in the organizational page in the Friday issue of the Jerusalem paper, "The Messiah's Shofar." Not every advance write-up of a lecture was of equal length. Prophets with deft elbows got longer notices and bigger headlines. Those with friends on the newspaper also got more fulsome articles. Those without know-how and friends "on the inside" got brief notices.

In addition to the newspaper articles, the speeches were announced in letters sent to the members of the branch. The announcements were written in two languages: Hebrew and Aramaic.

With each circular the member received a statement of his indebtedness to the branch with a stern reminder that if dues weren't paid, burial privileges in the cemetery on the Mount of Olives would be forfeited.

The lecture would be given in a hall in Solomon's Palace, which was maintained from rentals for meetings, conventions, Bar Mitzvahs and weddings.

The bus had already left the city with its lights and neon signs and was now moving in total darkness. What did a lecture of a prophet actually look like? I began thinking in concrete images. Suppose Isaiah was invited to lecture on the subject "My vision . . . "

The talk was scheduled for Sunday at 4:00 P.M. Promptly at that hour the prophet appeared, carrying with him his lecture notes. He arrived on a mule.

But the audience only began to assemble around 5:00 P.M. The chairman of the evening showed up at 5:45 P.M., and exactly at 6:00 he banged on the table with a wooden gavel, announcing: "Friends, after great exertions on our part we were successful in bringing to our branch one of our most popular prophets and lecturers, Jeremiah."

Secretary: "Not Jeremiah, Isaiah. Jeremiah was our speaker last Purim."

Chairman: "The secretary informs me that today's speaker is not Jeremiah, but Isaiah. He will speak to us on the subject, "What I saw in a Valley of Dry Bones."

Secretary: "No, the Valley of Dry Bones will be discussed next month by the Prophet Ezekiel. Today's speaker will deal with "The Vision of the Prophet Isaiah."

Chairman: "Before our guest gives his talk we will have a report from our cemetery committee."

Cemetery Chairman: "Our department had a very lively year. We arranged for 16 outstanding impressive funerals."

Secretary: "Not 16, but 15. Brother Hyrcanus is still alive."

Cemetery Chairman: "Yes, he's still breathing but he's been in a coma for four months and I think we can include him in this year's report."

Chairman: "Those who feel that we can include Brother Hyrcanus in the current year's report, please raise your hands."

It is passed unanimously.

Chairman: "Now we come to the talk by Nathan the Prophet."

Secretary: "Not Nathan, Isaiah. Nathan passed away."

Chairman: "Before the talk we have time for some announcements. Mr. Secretary."

Secretary: "I want to remind you that during the week of Sukkot we are planning a trip to Aram Neharaim. The total cost both ways on very comfortable two-humped camels will be one shekel. For wives, a half-shekel. For concubines, a quarter-shekel."

A Member: "Is there a limit on the number of concubines you can take?"

Secretary: "The maximum is six. The others you'll just have to leave home. Another important announcement: our branch has bought out an entire performance of the play, "The Sacrifice of Isaac." You must take your reservation early if you want good seats. And there's a deadline on reservations, after which no more tickets will be sold."

Chairman: "And now we come to our lecture to be given by Nathan the Prophet."

Secretary: "I told you Nathan passed away."

Chairman: "Before we hear from our cherished guest speaker, I want to make another announcement. Our branch is entitled to two delegates to our national convention. We always choose our delegates in democratic fashion, but this year to save time our executive officers picked two delegates and they are now en route to the convention. Is there anyone opposed to this action?"

No one was opposed.

Chairman: "That concludes our business meeting. Now we come to the main purpose of our gathering, the address by the Prophet Isaiah, who will tell us about a vision he had. (To Isaiah): How long is your lecture?"

Isaiah: "An hour."

Chairman: "Don't be a child. Who would sit an hour to listen to a vision?"

Isaiah: "Fifty minutes."

Chairman: "Cut it to 15."

Isaiah: "45."

Chairman: "20."

Isaiah: "40."

Chairman: "Remember, after you, we have a musical program, a Yemenite singer with a choir of Levites."

Isaiah: "A half hour."

Chairman (pounds table with gavel): "I will now make the absolutely final announcement. In the hall next to this one we have a buffet, with cold drinks and pastry. Those who would like to partake of the food may leave now, before the talk. We will lock the door after the talk has begun."

The entire audience got up and dashed to the exit. The entire audience, that is, except two old men too feeble to get out in time.

The Prophet Isaiah then went to the lectern and began: "The Vision of Isaiah the son of Amoz, which he saw concerning Judah and Jerusalem . . . "

The chairman quietly moved towards the lectern and on top of the prophet's notes he placed a large watch.

GLOSSARY

A<small>VEYRA</small>—sin, transgression.

B<small>AR</small> M<small>ITZVAH</small>—Ceremony in which a 13 year old boy assumes the duty of a man.

B<small>INTEL</small>—bundle.

B<small>OYREY</small> P<small>RI</small> H<small>AGOFEN</small>—a blessing recited while drinking wine. ("Blessed be the Creator of the fruit of wine)

C<small>HASID</small>—a pious man, disciple of a rabbi.

C<small>HOSHEVE</small> F<small>REIND</small>—Esteemed friends.

C<small>HOCHME</small>—a wise, clever remark.

C<small>HUTZPAH</small>—arrogance, cheek.

C<small>RUZEIRO</small>—Brazilian money.

E<small>IGHTEEN</small> B<small>LESSINGS</small>—solemn prayer containing eighteen blessings, recited in silence.

F<small>OLKSMENTCH</small>—an honest, simple, unpretentious man.

F<small>RINGES</small>—garment worn by pious Jews with four fringes at the four ends.

G<small>ENOSSE</small>—comrade.

H<small>ATIKVAH</small>—Jewish national anthem.

I<small>VRIT</small>—Hebrew.

K<small>HASENE</small>—wedding.

K<small>OL</small> N<small>IDREI</small>—Prayer recited on the eve of Yom Kippur.

K<small>REPLACH</small>—Dumplings, may contain chopped meat or cheese.

LANDSMAN—a man (or woman) from the same shtetel in the Old Country.

LANDMANSCHAFT—Society of such landsleit.

LITWO, OJCZYZNO MOJA—"Lithuania, my fatherland" (Polish), first line of the epic of the great Polish poet Adam Mickeiwicz.

MA SHLOMCHA—How are you? (Hebrew)

MATZO—unleavened bread eaten on the holiday of Pesach.

MEZUZA—Little oblong container attached to the right doorpost, containing a parchment with verses from Deuteronomy.

NACHES—joy, especially from achievements of a child.

NUDNIK—a bore, dullard.

OLOV HASHOLEM—"may he rest in peace" (Hebrew); words added after the name of a deceased person.

OSHAMNU, BOGADNU, GOZALNU—"We have sinned, falsified, robbed . . . " (Hebrew), First line of the prayer for the dying.

PESACH—Passover.

PURIM—Festival of Lots, commemorating the rescue of the Jews of Persia from Haman's plot.

REBETZIN—the wife of a rabbi.

REBOYNEY SHEL OYLEM—"Lord of the Universe" (Hebrew), one of God's names.

REFUAH SHLEYMA—a good recovery.

SHLIMAZEL—a loser.

SHTETEL—a small village.

SHTCAV—grass soup.

STIMMING—mood.

ROSSEL SOUP—chicken soup.

SEDER—ceremony observed on the first two nights (in Israel—on the first night only) of Passover.

SIMCHA—festival, joy.

SHAMES—sexton, beadle.

SHEKEL—old biblical coin.

Sнема Iѕroel—"Hear, Oh, God" (Hebrew); The most common Hebrew prayer recited three or four times a day; last prayer uttered on death bed.

Sukkoтн—Festival of Tabernacles.

Yiddishkeit—Spiritual content of Jewish life.

Yom Kippur—Most solemn of Jewish holidays.

GLOSSARY—NAMES

ASCH, SHALOM—Yiddish writer, (1880-1957).

BERGELSON, DAVID—Soviet Yiddish writer, (1884-1952).

BIALIK, CHAIM NACHMAN—One of the most prominent Hebrew poets, (1873-1934).

HALPERN, MOYSHE LEYB—Yiddish American poet, (1886-1932).

HALEVI, YEHUDA—Great Hebrew poet of the Middle Ages. Born 1085, Toledo, Spain; died 1140, Palestine.

LEIWICK, H.—Yiddish poet and dramatist, (1888-1962).

MANGER, ITZIK—Yiddish folks-poet, (1901-1969).

MENDELE, MOYCHER SEFORIM—"Grandfather" of Yiddish literature, (1836-1917).

NADIR, MOYSHE—One of the outstanding Yiddish satirist, and poets, (1885-1943).

RAISIN, ABRAHAM—Yiddish poet, (1876-1953).

SCHNEYUR, ZALMEN—Yiddish-Hebrew writer and poet, (1887-1959).

STERN, ISROEL—Mystical Yiddish poet, perished in the ghetto of Warsaw, 1942.